London
Curiosities

To three lovely ladies – Amelia, Beau and Scarlett –
my very special granddaughters.

London
Curiosities

The Capital's Odd and Obscure, Weird and Wonderful Places

John Wade

PEN & SWORD
HISTORY

First published in Great Britain in 2017 by
Pen & Sword History
an imprint of
Pen & Sword Books Ltd
47 Church Street
Barnsley
South Yorkshire
S70 2AS

ISBN 978 1 47387 911 9

A CIP catalogue record for this book is available from the British
Library

Typeset in Ehrhardt by
Mac Style Ltd, Bridlington, East Yorkshire
Printed and bound in the UK by CPI Group (UK) Ltd,
Croydon, CR0 4YY

Pen & Sword Books Ltd incorporates the imprints of Pen &
Sword Archaeology, Atlas, Aviation, Battleground, Discovery,
Family History, History, Maritime, Military, Naval, Politics,
Railways, Select, Transport, True Crime, Fiction, Frontline
Books, Leo Cooper, Praetorian Press, Seaforth Publishing and
Wharncliffe.

For a complete list of Pen & Sword titles please contact
PEN & SWORD BOOKS LIMITED
47 Church Street, Barnsley, South Yorkshire, S70 2AS, England
E-mail: enquiries@pen-and-sword.co.uk
Website: www.pen-and-sword.co.uk

Contents

Introduction

Every day, thousands of Londoners walk past Cleopatra's Needle on the north bank of the river Thames. But how many of those who stroll along the Thames Embankment without giving the monument a second glance, pause to wonder how a 3,000-year-old Ancient Egyptian obelisk came to be here in modern-day London? How many are aware of the dramatic and dangerous journey it made to get to England? Who knows that it actually has very little to do with Cleopatra?

Across the road from Cleopatra's Needle, in a small ornamental garden, there is a huge and impressively ornate gateway that leads to absolutely nothing. Nearby, embedded into the wall of the embankment that skirts the river there is a modest memorial to a man who took on a monumental task in the nineteenth century. There is a strong connection between the memorial and the gateway, but what is it?

Up the road, opposite the Houses of Parliament, there's a plaque on a wall dedicated to the man who invented the first traffic lights, which exploded soon after they were erected on this spot. Across Westminster Bridge stands a statue of a lion made of a material whose exact composition has never been revealed. Turn left from here and you'll find the last visible remains of an amazing exhibition whose memory today has been all but lost. Turn right and you'll come to a bridge where there are tall obelisks with incongruously carved pineapples on their tops. Further on, a statue on the next bridge holds a miniature model of St Paul's Cathedral.

These are all within walking distance of each other. Unsurprisingly, you can find a great many more similar oddities spread out across the 600 square miles of the capital. Some, like those just mentioned, are there in plain sight, easy to see, but with origins that are often difficult to figure out. Others are hidden away in places you would never know about unless you knew where to look.

Who knew that beneath the Albert Memorial there is an undercroft that resembles a church crypt? Or that there are catacombs under Camden? Who would expect to find a lighthouse in East London, sphinxes in South London, dummy houses in West London, or a tomb whose design influenced the iconic red telephone box in North London?

If things like this fascinate you, then you are ready to begin your journey through London, to learn fresh facts about places you might previously have taken for granted and to discover new places, objects, monuments and many other peculiarities that you never even knew existed in this Capital of Curiosities.

Chapter 1

Strangeness in the Streets

London's streets are full of strangeness. Search them out and items from the past can be unexpectedly found everywhere, from remnants of lost buildings, to chimneys rising from pavements, noses sticking out of walls, unexplained signs attached to buildings and even a Russian tank on a street corner.

* * *

The Last Post

Britain's General Post Office headquarters, the country's first purpose-built post office, was erected at St Martin's Le Grand in the City of London between 1825 and 1829. Designed by Robert Smirke, an English architect who was known as one of the leaders of the Greek Revival style, it was an enormous building, 400 feet long and 80 feet deep.

The Grecian style included huge porches flanked by pillars whose tops displayed spiral scroll-like ornamentation, with a triangular pediment topping off the central columns. It was the kind of building that might have looked more at home on a hilltop outside Athens than at the side of a busy London City road.

This magnificent building was closed in 1910 and demolished in 1912. But one small piece still remains. It stands in a street in Walthamstow outside the Vestry House Museum in Vestry Road. The museum, whose building once housed the parish workhouse and which has also been a police station and private house, now contains exhibits that show the history of the London Borough of Waltham Forest.

The General Post Office building, which was demolished in 1912.

The last remains of the old Post Office building might be small in comparison to the entire edifice, but on its own it still dominates the street. It is actually the top part, or capital, of one of the fluted columns that so characterised the look of the old Post Office. When the building was being demolished, this small yet significant lump of stone was purchased by a stonemason named Frank Mortimer, who presented it to the Borough of Walthamstow. It was shifted to its present location in 1954 from its original site in nearby Lloyd Park, today home to the William Morris house and gardens.

The last remains of the old Post Office building, now in a Walthamstow street.

* * *

Unexpected Chimneys

The place for a chimney is on the roof of a building – unless of course it is discovered sprouting from a pavement or from the balustrade of a bridge …

The Albert Hall chimney

On a small traffic island in the middle of Kensington Gore, no more than a few walking steps south-west of the Royal Albert Hall, there stands a tall, slender brick-built chimney whose height dwarfs the surrounding buildings.

The chimney, whose base is at pavement level, was designed by Major General Henry Young Darracott Scott RE, the principal architect of the Royal Albert Hall. When the concert hall opened in 1871, a large conservatory was attached to its south entrance. This marked the north end of the South Kensington Royal Horticultural Society, which was founded in 1804 to allow members to present papers on horticultural activities and discoveries.

To heat the vast conservatory, boilers were positioned below street level. In the same basement, further boilers were built to heat the interior of the Royal Albert Hall, and both sets of boilers

The chimney behind the Royal Albert Hall.

shared a common chimney, which was replaced by the present one in 1884. Five years later, the conservatory was demolished, but the chimney standing outside the Royal Albert Hall today is still used as the outlet for the hall's steam boilers. It is a Grade I listed structure.

The Tower Bridge chimney

Lamp posts line the balustrades each side of the roadway of Tower Bridge. But if you look carefully at one at the north end of the bridge, you'll notice it looks a little different from all the others. Although it is similar in style to neighbouring lamp posts, it doesn't actually support a lamp. This is because, in reality, it's a chimney.

Beneath the bridge there is a room, once used by the Royal Fusiliers, whose guards protected the Tower of London. The room had a coal fire and the smoke from that was fed out to the chimney on the bridge, which was disguised as best it could be as a lamp post.

The chimney is no longer in operation, since coal fires are not permitted in London these days. They were outlawed in 1956 with the introduction of the Clean Air Act, which decreed that only smokeless fuel could be used for fires in certain smokeless zones of the country. The Act's introduction followed London's Great Smog of 1952.

The chimney disguised as a lamp post that stands on Tower Bridge.

* * *

Sewer Lamps

In nineteenth-century London, many of the gas lamps were created for a double purpose. The first was to obviously light the streets. The second was to burn off smelly and germ-ridden gases from the sewers. The Patent Sewer Gas Lamp was invented by Birmingham inventor Joseph Webb. One still remains today in a road off the Strand in central London.

The process involved methane gas being collected by small domes in the sewers, from where it was diverted to the lamps in the streets above. It was rare that the methane was enough to completely power the lamps, which were also fed by ordinary town gas supplies. When the town gas had burnt enough to heat the lamp's filament to the right temperature, the methane gas was automatically drawn from the sewers.

The last remaining sewer gas destructor lamp in Westminster can still be seen burning day and night, and although the post is a replica, the lantern at the top is the original. A sign adjacent to the lamp explains that it was installed in association with Sir Joseph Bazalgette's revolutionary Victorian Embankment sewer, which opened in 1870, and that it continues to burn today off residual biogas. (Biogas is produced from raw materials such as agricultural waste, manure, municipal waste, plant material, sewage, green waste or food waste.)

The Carting Lane sewer lamp, still burning after all these years.

The lamp is in a street called Carting Lane, a tempting name for graffiti artists who, in appreciation of the gas that originally fuelled the lamp, need to be discouraged from changing the 'C' in the street name to 'F'.

* * *

Noses On Walls

Admiralty Arch stands magnificently between Trafalgar Square and the Mall, serving as an entrance to the road that leads to Buckingham Palace. It consists of five arches: two for pedestrians, two for vehicular traffic and a central one that is opened only for ceremonial occasions. The Arch was commissioned by King Edward VII and dedicated to his mother, Queen Victoria.

The nose that protrudes from a wall in Admiralty Arch.

Approaching the Arch from the Trafalgar Square side, and entering the arch on the right, about 7 feet from the ground, there is a nose protruding from the wall. All kinds of stories and legends have grown up about this small and rather strange sculpture.

One story is that it is a spare nose for the statue of Nelson that stands nearby at the top of the nearly 170 feet high column in Trafalgar Square. Another rumour is that it was placed there to mock Napoleon, who was said to have had a large nose. It is also said that, being waist-height to a rider on a horse, it was once tweaked for luck by members of the cavalry troupers from nearby Horse Guard's Parade as they passed through the arch.

The stories are pure myth. The nose was actually installed within the arch in 1997. It was created by artist Richard Buckley in reaction to debates at that time about the invasion of privacy by closed circuit TV cameras around London.

Buckley's inspiration was the Situationists, a group of artistic social revolutionaries who were prominent in Europe from the late 1950s until the early 1970s. His aim was to install his nose sculptures under the noses of the cameras without being detected – and Admiralty Arch was not the only location for his prank. The sculptures were modelled on the artist's own nose, and originally there were about thirty-five of them, attached to the National Gallery, Tate Britain and various buildings in and around Soho. It is said that if you can track down and touch all of the existing noses, you will attain great wealth.

* * *

The Wherryman's Seat

Until 1750, when a bridge was built across the Thames at Westminster, the only way to cross the river was via London Bridge. Consequently, a trade grew up for watermen to taxi passengers across the river in small boats. While they waited for fares and for their boats to fill up, the operators sat on rough stone benches, and one still exists today. It is set into a wall on the South Bank of the Thames, in Bear Gardens, close to Southwark Bridge.

The boats at this time were known as wherries, a name given to both light craft such as small rowing boats or larger boats used for fishing. The men who operated them were known, in the eighteenth century, not as ferrymen, but as wherrymen.

The seat used by wherrymen or ferrymen.

The south bank of the Thames at this time was a lawless place, and Bear Gardens is named after London's last bear baiting pit, which was situated here. The area was also known for its brothels, the stink of its open sewers and the toxic smells from nearby tanneries. The banks of the river were muddy, rat infested and disease ridden. It was, in short, an extremely insalubrious place in which to find yourself.

Anne Perrys WM Monk Series description

The wherryman's seat that still exists doesn't show much in the way of luxury for those who occupied it, being little more than a hard, narrow bench made of flint. The life of a wherryman, or ferryman, who sat here waiting for passengers, many of whom would have been drunk and unruly, wasn't for the faint-hearted.

* * *

The London Cholera Pump

Broadwick Street in Soho is home to an ancient water pump, the original of which proved to be the origins of one of London's worst outbreaks of cholera. The disease, which is the result of infection of the small intestine by a bacterium, was rife in London during the nineteenth century. According to popular opinion of the time, contagion was airborne and spread by bad smells in the air – of which there were plenty in London at this time.

In 1854, a London physician named John Snow carried out researches that proved otherwise. In that year, nearly 11,000 Londoners died of cholera. Snow studied the cases of 500 or so victims, all of whom lived in, or had connections with, Soho. It led

The replica of the cholera pump still standing today near the John Snow pub.

to identifying the water pump in what was then Broad Street, now Broadwick Street, as the source of the disease.

It transpired that sewage from a nearby cesspit had been leaking into the pump's water system. Snow had the handle of the pump removed and the cases of cholera in the area immediately diminished. Although initially treated as dubious, his researches eventually proved that the sewage-contaminated water coming from the pump was the true cause of the disease.

The pump that can still be seen in Broadwick Street is a replica of the original, which is thought to have stood outside a nearby pub. The pub's name, appropriately enough, is the John Snow.

Interestingly, not everyone who had contracted the disease from the pump actually lived in the area. Some actually travelled many miles to obtain their water supply from the pump because they favoured its taste over water from other pumps!

* * *

Cannons that Became Bollards

Many ancient bollards in the streets of London look a lot like the barrels of cannons that have been erected vertically. This is because many of them really were cannon barrels – and those that weren't, were replicas of those that were.

The idea stems from 1805, when the Royal Navy defeated the French and the Spanish at the Battle of Trafalgar. It was a victory that the British were determined to flaunt as much as possible. The story goes that following the battle, the British began stripping the French boats of their valuables. Anything that could be retrofitted to the British fleet of ships was soon purloined and adapted.

At this point, urban myth enters the story. Many believe that the cannons on the French vessels proved to be too big for British ships. So they were dismantled and their barrels were distributed around East

The South London street bollard that is reputed to be the remains of a French Cannon from the Battle of Trafalgar.

London where, used as bollards, they were placed on street corners to prevent the iron wheels of carts and carriages from causing damage. The idea became so popular that, when the supply of cannons ran out, replicas of the originals were made and the French cannon barrel became the model for bollards everywhere throughout the streets of not just London, but elsewhere throughout Britain.

Few remain today, and even fewer of the originals have survived. But one that is widely reckoned to be from an original French ship's cannon can still be seen at Bankside on the South Bank of the Thames, close to Shakespeare's Globe Theatre.

Even today, bollards are still made to resemble the barrels of cannons. Mostly, however, the modern versions have rounded tops that simulate a cannon ball being placed into the cannon's mouth. The original surviving French cannon bollard on the South Bank is devoid of this ornamentation.

The most famous celebration of the Battle of Trafalgar victory is, of course, Trafalgar Square in London, dominated by Nelson's column. Trafalgar Square was not opened until 1844, thirty-nine years after the battle that it commemorates, but here too metal captured from French ships was put to good use, as bronze relief panels on the pedestal of Nelson's Column.

* * *

The Russian Tank in South London

On the corner of Mandela Way and Pages Walk in Bermondsey there is a small patch of wasteland, on which stands a full-size, genuine, Russian tank.

The story goes that the land is owned by a local property developer who lost a battle with Southwark Council when he wanted to build a house on the plot. His reaction was to apply for planning permission to put a tank on the land. The council, assuming he meant some kind of water container, granted permission, and the developer promptly responded by putting a decommissioned T34 Soviet Army tank on the spot.

South London's Russian tank.

That was in 1995, and it has been there ever since, regularly painted by graffiti and other local artists in a variety of colours and styles, ranging from its natural gunmetal to pink, yellow and orange, taking in stripes, psychedelic patterns and much else along the way.

The tank was originally brought to London from Czechoslovakia, where it had been in service. It was purchased by a film company, making an updated version of Shakespeare's *Richard III*, which was filmed, among other locations, at Battersea Power Station. When the filming ended, the tank was sold to a scrap dealer, who sold it on to the South London property developer.

According to the council, no such planning permission paperwork exists – unlike the tank, which is indisputably real.

* * *

The Duke of Wellington's Horse Block

On the edge of the pavement outside number 107 Pall Mall, there are two stones, a short stone on top of a longer one. They are there because the Duke of Wellington requested them to be placed in this position in 1830, at a time when he had been Prime Minister for two years.

The horse block used by the Duke of Wellington.

The building in front of which the stones stand is the Athenaeum Club, a private members' club that opened its doors in 1824. The Duke of Wellington was a member, as were, over the years, such luminaries as Charles Darwin, Charles Dickens, Sir Arthur Conan Doyle, Cecil Rhodes and Sir Winston Churchill.

The stones, which go relatively unnoticed today, were erected to allow the Duke of Wellington to easily mount and dismount his horse when visiting the club. They were known then as a horse block.

* * *

Getting the Measure of Trafalgar Square

In 1834, a government decision to dispose of two cartloads of tally sticks, part of an ancient accounting system no longer in use, led to the unwise decision to burn them in stoves situated in a basement under the House of Lords. As a result, in the early evening of 16 October that year, fire erupted and ignited panelling in the House of Lords before spreading through the House of Commons, and with the exception of a few buildings, decimating the Palace of Westminster.

Among the many valuable items lost in the fire were the standards of the Imperial units of measurement. It meant that there was no longer a criterion by which to confirm the actual dimensions of inches, feet and yards, as well as some of the more obscure units of measurement in use at the time.

To rectify that, astronomer and mathematician George Airy was asked to create new standard units of measurement. It took him four years, and to ensure that the measurements were never lost again, they were set in brass, triplicated, and in 1876, embedded in three London landmarks. One set of measurements is to be found in the Great Hall of the Guildhall; the second beside the gates of the Royal Observatory in Greenwich; and the third in steps on the north side of Trafalgar Square, leading up to the National Gallery.

Set in stone in Trafalgar Square: the official units of Imperial measure.

Today, it's interesting to look at these ancient measurements embedded in the stone steps in Trafalgar Square and remember just how complicated they were, compared to the simplicity of today's metric system. Those who were brought up on Imperial measurements will undoubtedly recall that there were 12 inches to the foot and 3 feet to the yard. But how many remember that there were 22 yards to the chain, 10 chains to the furlong and 8 furlongs to the mile? There was also a little less than 8 inches to the link and 100 links to the chain. Rod, pole and perch were three names for the same measurement, which measured 5½ yards. The British have always been good at making life difficult for themselves.

* * *

London's Last Kiln

At Walmer Road, close to Pottery Lane in North Kensington, amid the upmarket houses that typify the area, there stands a large, round brick building that appears totally out of place. It is the last example of a kiln left in London.

The kiln dates back to the nineteenth century, when the soil in this area was mostly composed of clay, which led to the area being dominated by brick fields. This was a time when there was an increasing need for bricks to build houses in the growing suburbs.

The kiln, in North Kensington.

The bricks were fired in the kiln still standing here and stored in sheds along Pottery Lane. The whole area at the time was a huge slum in which the brick makers lived alongside pig keepers who had been moved west from their homes around Marble Arch as London expanded.

The area was known as the Potteries and Piggeries – a far cry from the respectable location that it later became. Today, only the kiln remains as a reminder of a very different way of life in this now far more salubrious area.

* * *

How Soldiers Helped the Trembling Lady

If you happen to be commanding a troop of soldiers crossing the Albert Bridge from Chelsea to Battersea, or the other way around, you should ensure that your soldiers break step as they make the crossing. That's what notices at each end of the bridge advise.

Albert Bridge was built as a suspension bridge, which helps to make it one of the most attractive bridges in London. But the design also means that it is one of the most delicate, and it has had an unfortunate tendency to vibrate as traffic crosses it since its opening in 1873. Consequently, very early in its life, it acquired the nickname of The Trembling Lady.

Vibrations caused by soldiers marching in step across the bridge were of particular concern, and since Chelsea Barracks was nearby, this was a regular occurrence when the bridge was first built. Prior to the Albert Bridge being opened, similar styles of bridge in England and France had collapsed in 1831 and 1850, and in an endeavour to counteract a similar tragedy happening in London, signs were erected

Warning signs to soldiers on Albert Bridge.

advising soldiers to break step, rather than marching to a set rhythm, as they crossed the bridge, to help reduced the vibrations.

With the Chelsea Barracks closing in 2008, there is less chance today of tragedy befalling the bridge due to marching soldiers, but the signs remain, stating: 'All troops must break step when marching over this bridge.'

* * *

London's First Drinking Fountain

Set into the railings of the splendidly named St Sepulchre-without-Newgate church near Holborn Viaduct, there is a small drinking fountain. But this isn't just any drinking fountain. It was the very first to be erected in London at a time when it, and those that followed,

London's first drinking fountain.

were the only safe places for people to obtain water truly suitable for drinking.

By the mid-nineteenth century, it was so well known that water in general was polluted and prone to spreading disease that most accepted that it was safer to drink beer. In 1852, the Metropolis Water

Act made it illegal for water supply companies to draw their water from the Thames, which was polluted with raw sewage.

In 1859, banker and Member of Parliament Samuel Gurney, along with politician Edward Wakefield, formed the *Metropolitan Drinking Fountain and Cattle Trough Association*. Its purpose was to provide clean, free water for both people and animals.

Over the course of six years, the Association built more than eighty drinking fountains, as well as cattle troughs. The one outside St Sepulchre-without-Newgate church was the first, and at its height, was reckoned to be used by about 7,000 people every day.

The *Metropolitan Drinking Fountain and Cattle Trough Association* still exists today. Under the rather less grand name of the Drinking Fountain Association, it still provides drinking fountains where they are needed.

* * *

Mendelssohn's Tree

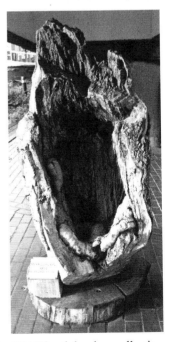

If you'd like to see a piece of the tree under which Mendelssohn is reputed to have sat, gaining inspiration for such pieces of music as *A Midsummer Night's Dream*, the place to go, appropriately enough, is to the Barbican Concert Hall.

The Barbican Centre was opened in 1982. But more than a century before, in 1880, ancient woodland, known as Burnham Beaches in Buckinghamshire, was purchased for the nation by the Corporation of London. It is said that the composer Mendelssohn enjoyed visiting the woodland and often sat under the tree, part of which can now be found on the Barbican's Highwalk. It was reclaimed from the ancient woodland and erected here following a storm in 1990.

Did Mendelssohn really sit under the tree from which this piece was taken?

* * *

The Police Coat Hook

In Great Newport Street, close to Covent Garden, you'll find a small coat hook sticking out of a wall. But you had better not hang your coat on it, because a sign above the hook claims it for the Metropolitan Police.

The police coat hook in Great Newport Street.

The hook has been there since the 1930s, in the days when policemen wore traditional helmets and donned capes to protect them from wet weather. Being a busy area where several roads converged, a policeman was usually on duty back in those days to direct traffic.

Such policemen, needing somewhere to hang their capes, opted for a simple nail in the wall of a nearby building, until a builder renovating the property took it upon himself to provide something a little more substantial and stylish. Hence the Metropolitan Police official coat hook was produced and installed.

* * *

Fire Plaques

Following the Great Fire of London in 1666, insurance companies began to form to help those whose houses might be damaged or destroyed by fire. Householders would pay a premium and be given a metal plaque to be mounted outside their homes.

There was no official fire brigade at this time, but rather a number of independent brigades, each of which worked for its own insurance company. If a house caught fire, any number of private brigades might arrive to help. But if the house did not display a plaque belonging to their designated insurance company, they would turn away again and let it burn. Only the brigade associated with the relevant insurance company's plaque would stay to fight the fire.

The metal plaques were known as firemarks and some can still be seen mounted on ancient buildings around the capital.

This rather haphazard and heartless way of dealing with fires was improved upon in 1833, when ten independent fire insurance companies amalgamated to form the London Fire Engine Establishment. Its director was James Braidwood, who had already formed the country's first municipal fire service in Edinburgh in 1824. He died in 1861 while helping to fight a warehouse fire at Tooley Street, often referred to as the greatest fire since the Great Fire of London nearly 200 years before.

Fire marks, which can still be seen in and around London. These six examples were discovered in Highgate, Highbury, Lambeth, Spitalfields and Greenwich.

* * *

The Swinging Shop Signs of Lombard Street

Lombard Street in the City of London is the place to go to see advertising signs that would have been common in the seventeenth and eighteenth centuries. Although mainly replicas made in the Edwardian era, these date back to the days when the street was home to London's goldsmiths. It was a time when businesses used signs like these to advertise their trades, and since a good percentage of the population could neither read nor write, their advertising took the form of visual images.

Today, a stroll down Lombard Street reveals what's left of more than 150 signs that once swung above the doors of shops, protruded out into the roadway or were fixed to posts in front of houses.

Among those that still exist is a huge golden grasshopper, once part of the family crest of English merchant and financier Sir Thomas Gresham, whose family built the Royal Exchange and who lived in the house the sign still adorns. Elsewhere you'll see a cat playing a fiddle and what appears to be the head of King Charles II with a sun above it.

Although the signs originally referred to the people or businesses that occupied the associated premises, the connection between the sign's contents and the nature of the business was not always obvious. A sign showing a bugle indicated a Post Office; a unicorn meant an apothecary; Adam and Eve were indications of a fruiterer, and most incongruous of all, a spotted cat might stand outside a perfumer's shop – because a popular perfume of the day was obtained from the anal glands of African cat-like creatures called civets!

Trading signs still found today in Lombard Street.

Two signs, once to be found in Lombard Street but no longer in place, were the origins of logos used by two notable banks today: namely a black spreadeagle and a black horse, now the emblems of Barclays and Lloyds banks.

* * *

The Narrowest Alley

Walking along St Martin's Lane, a little way north of Trafalgar Square, it's easy to miss an extremely narrow opening next door to the Coliseum Theatre. This is Brydges Place and its claim to fame is that it is the narrowest alley in London.

Fairly long and very claustrophobic in places, it runs to Bedfordbury in Covent Garden. At its narrowest point, it measures no more than 15 inches, making it impossible for two people to pass.

One side of the alley is formed by the back of a pub called The Marquis of Granby, said to be a popular haunt of the novelist Charles Dickens.

Brydges Place is London's narrowest alley.

Chapter 2

Weird Houses

Over the years, people have built and lived in some of the weirdest houses in London: large, small, thin and narrow – and some buildings that look like houses are not even houses at all. Here's a round-up of just some the strangest houses, all of which can be seen on a trip around the capital.

*   *   *

The Best Address In London

The most prestigious address, not just in London, but in the whole of the UK, must surely be No. 1 London. Unfortunately, this iconic address doesn't actually exist. It's merely the nickname given to Apsley House, whose true address is 149 Piccadilly, Hyde Park Corner.

Apsley House was built in 1778 for Lord Apsley, the then current Lord Chancellor. From 1817, it was the home of the Duke of Wellington, granted to him by a grateful nation in recognition of his defeat of Napoleon at the Battle of Waterloo in 1815. Today, it is a Grade I listed building, run by British Heritage as a museum and art gallery, open to the public.

Apsley House, near Hyde Park Corner, also known as No. 1 London.

But back in the eighteenth century, when the house was built by neoclassical architect Robert Adam, it stood on a toll road at the very point where Central London started, which made it the first house in London. Hence the nickname by which it was soon known.

* * *

Bayswater's Dummy Houses

From the front, the dummy houses look like the real thing.

From the back, the houses are revealed as dummies.

Leinster Gardens in West London's Bayswater is a road of elegant five-storey houses. Columns flank impressive entrances and balconies front windows on all but the top floors. All the houses in the terrace share a similar style, but two are not what they seem.

Take a closer look at numbers 23 and 24 and it becomes evident that there are no curtains or any kind of internal decoration behind them. In fact, every window is completely blocked, and if it were possible to try entering the houses, it would soon be discovered that the front doors did not open. The reason for this is that, despite the fact that the two buildings share the style and ornamentation found in the rest of the terrace, they are dummy houses.

Take a walk around the block, into Porchester Gardens, which runs parallel to Leinster Gardens, look over a high brick wall towards the back of numbers 23 and 24 and what you see is a flat façade rather like the back of a film set, and in front of that, a huge gap that falls away below the level of the road and the gardens of surrounding houses to reveal twin tracks of the London Underground. Girders are strung across the gap behind the flat front of the dummy houses and between the gardens of the genuine houses to prevent the buildings on either side collapsing into the gap. The reason for this dates back to 1860, when the first underground railways were built in London.

With steam trains being the only practical method of pulling carriages at the time, a method needed to be found that did not involve fumes from engines suffocating passengers as the engines ejected steam and sulphurous smoke in the way they did above ground. So new condensing engines were developed, in which steam was diverted from the usual exhaust system, to be condensed and delivered back into the water tanks, thus emitting less steam. That which did need to be exhausted was discharged when the trains emerged briefly into the open before plunging back into the tunnels.

To allow for this, two houses were demolished in Leinster Gardens and the fake facades built to link the terrace on each side to give the impression of one continuous row of houses. The space behind them was left empty and uncovered as a place for the trains to vent their steam. Today, the underground trains are electric, but the gap in the terrace of houses in Leinster Gardens remains.

* * *

The Smallest House in London

Several buildings have claimed to be the smallest house in London, but the one usually recognised as the most likely to be worthy of the title is at 10 Hyde Park Place, near Marble Arch. Built in 1805, it is a mere 3 feet 6 inches wide.

The house was built across an alley between two buildings that led to St George's Graveyard, and it is generally thought that it was erected to deter grave robbers from using the right of way to enter the graveyard. Inside, it is little more than a passage between the front and back, with one single bedroom above it.

Writer and film producer Lewis Grant Wallace, born in 1910, was the one and only known tenant of the house. Despite being so small, it was bombed in 1941, during the Second World War.

* * *

The Narrowest House in London

Laying claim to be the narrowest house in London, No. 110 Goldhawk Road in Shepherd's Bush, built in the 1870s, was once a hat shop and is now a privately owned house. Slotted into an alley between two shops, it is built on five levels and measures just 5 feet 6 inches wide.

A lower floor contains the kitchen with a door to the garden. There is a reception room on the ground floor with two rooms on the first floor, bedroom and shower on the second floor and a further bedroom on the top floor.

In 2009, due to the high demand for housing in London, it sold for £550,000.

* * *

The narrow house at 110 Goldhawk Road.

The Thinnest House in London

Where Thurloe Square meets South Terrace in Knightsbridge stands what is probably the thinnest house in London. Wedge-shaped and standing at the end of a terrace, it is little more than 7 feet wide at its eastern end, although it widens out to about 34 feet at its western boundary with the house next door.

It appears to have been built this way to follow the line of adjacent railway tracks.

* * *

The remarkably thin house in Knightsbridge.

The Oldest House in the City

As every good history scholar knows, the Great Fire of London swept through the City in September 1666, destroying nearly everything in its path. It was estimated that the inferno destroyed more than 13,000 houses, nearly ninety churches and most of the City's authority buildings. But one house survived, and today it is reckoned to be the oldest in the City of London.

The house stands at what is now 41–42 Cloth Fair in Farringdon. It was completed in 1614, only two years before the fire broke out, and survived because it was built inside a large group of priory walls.

The house in Cloth Fair that survived the Great Fire of London.

Tragically, it was very nearly demolished in 1929 as part of a sanitary scheme. It was saved, however, and today survives largely thanks to owners who purchased and refurbished it 1995. In the year 2000, it was awarded a City Heritage Award, a prestigious honor given annually to the best refurbishment project in the City.

* * *

St Bartholomew's Gatehouse

During the First World War, a German Zeppelin bombing raid damaged what was thought to be a Georgian shop front in West Smithfield. As the false front of the building fell away, evidence of a much older building was discovered beneath the rather bland surface. After the war, the building was restored, the work being completed in 1932, to reveal St Bartholomew's Gatehouse in all its Tudor glory.

The lower half of the structure is a gatehouse formed by a thirteenth-century arch, which originally led to St Bartholomew-the-Great, a priory founded in 1123. Much of that building was destroyed during Henry VIII's dissolution of the monasteries, as part of his reformation of Tudor England.

The arch, however, remained, and in 1595, a local resident built a house on top of it, comprising two storeys, the upper one slightly overhanging the lower one, and with a small attic above. A statue of Saint Bartholomew still stands between the two upper windows.

Legend once had it that Queen Mary I ate chicken and drank wine while sitting in the house as she watched protestant martyrs being burnt at the stake outside. It is true that many London martyrs were burnt at nearby Spitalfields, but Queen Mary died about forty years before the house above the arch was even built.

Along with a house in Cloth Fair, generally regarded as the oldest house in London, this was one of the very few buildings that survived the Great Fire of London.

The bland Georgian façade was added sometime during the eighteenth century, covering the original Tudor architecture, which remained hidden until the Zeppelin raid whose bomb uncovered the beauty of the house beneath.

* * *

Mr Duck of Duck Island

On an island in the middle of a lake in St James's Park there stands a small house. The piece of land it occupies, surrounded by a garden, is called Duck Island, the house is called Duck Cottage, and back in the eighteenth century, it was occupied by an English poet named Stephen Duck, also known as the Thresher Poet. The name referred to what was regarded as his best poem, *The Thresher's Labour*, inspired by his humble background as an agricultural labourer.

The island got its name from the wild birds that have lived there right back to the times when the area was part of Henry VIII's hunting

Duck Cottage on Duck Island in St James's Park.

grounds. When, in the seventeenth century, Charles II decreed that the land should be laid out as a park, a decoy was built for nesting birds. It comprised a system of channels surrounding the piece of land that became known as Duck Island, and the king created the post of Governor of Duck Island to look after it.

A century later, in 1733, the post was revived by Queen Caroline and the title was bestowed again, this time, appropriately enough, on Stephen Duck. Unfortunately, in 1771, the island was swept away.

Another half a century went past, and in 1827, the park was redesigned and Duck Island once again came to prominence. In 1840, the Ornithological Society of London sought permission to build a house on the island as a residence for a bird keeper. Duck Cottage was built.

For a while, Duck Cottage was a popular landmark of the park. Later, it slid into obscurity. From 1900, it was occupied by an official Bird Keeper, but abandoned in 1953. It was remodelled and extended in 1959 and fully restored in 1982.

Today, Duck Cottage is owned by the London Historic Parks and Gardens Trust, which is concerned chiefly with the protection and enhancement of St James's Park.

* * *

Southwark's Upside Down House

Just over Blackfriars Bridge and a little way along Blackfriars Road, there is a house that appears to have been built upside down. At the top, there is an upside down shop with window, doorway and a sign proclaiming it to be the premises of Engineers and Furnishers W.H. Willcox & Co Ltd. Below that, down to the pavement, there are three storeys of windows with their sills at the top and lintels below.

It's actually not a house at all. It's the front of an old building dating back to the 1780s, when it was used as a storage place for carriages and a facility for horses. The upside down façade is the work of artist Alex Chinneck, who enjoys working on large-scale projects such as a house in Kent that appears to have slid down into its front garden.

The illusion was created using flattened bricks and polystyrene. The sign above (or below) the shop front is genuine. It was discovered by the artist in a Welsh scrapyard and he felt that it suited his upside down house perfectly. The artist called his work *Miner on the Moon*.

The house, or gigantic piece of artwork, might or might not last much longer. At the time of writing, the area was due for demolition – but it was fun while it lasted.

The upside down house in Blackfriars Road.

Chapter 3

Surprising Buildings

London abounds with surprising buildings whose fascinating histories date back to Victorian times and earlier. Some are all that remain of far grander edifices no longer in existence; others are individual buildings that have survived down the ages to be turned today into something very different from their original purposes. All have interesting stories to tell.

* * *

London's Smallest Police Station

The smallest police station in London is also the smallest in Britain. It stands in Trafalgar Square – and it looks nothing like any kind of building, let alone a police station. It resembles, in fact, a rather ornate lamp post, which isn't surprising, since that is what it originally was.

Back in the 1920s, police boxes were scattered around the London streets. They took the form of rectangular blue boxes, each with a telephone linked to the nearest police station accessed behind a small door in the front of the box, for use by officers patrolling the area. In emergencies, members the public were also entitled to use the telephone, while

London's smallest police station, in Trafalgar Square.

a light on the top would flash to alert the nearest police officer that he or she should contact the station. Inside there was enough room for a police officer to take a break, make necessary telephone calls or handle paperwork.

One such police box, situated outside Trafalgar Square tube station in the early 1920s, was due to be renovated, but was instead scrapped due to public objections. It was felt, however, that some kind of police presence and means of communication should remain in the area to watch out for troublesome protesters who often used Trafalgar Square for their demonstrations.

In 1926, the large rotund plinth that held the street light at the south-east corner of the Square was hollowed out, and then fitted with doors and very narrow windows. From inside, a police officer could carry out covert scrutiny of Trafalgar Square. The officer also had access to a telephone linked directly to Scotland Yard, and when the telephone was in use, the lamp on top flashed to alert any nearby police officers to possible trouble. In an emergency, the tiny round building could also accommodate two prisoners. There is a legend, never actually proved, that the lamp on top of the small building came from Nelson's flagship HMS *Victory*.

Today, London's smallest police station is still in use, but only by council cleaners who store their brooms in it.

* * *

London's Smallest Church

Squeezed between two large office buildings in Bishopsgate is what most reckon to be the smallest church in London. St Ethelburga the Virgin was founded in the thirteenth century. Its name comes from its dedication to the abbess of Barking Abbey in the seventh century.

The church was rebuilt in the fifteenth century, and a small square bell turret was added in the eighteenth century. Inside it comprises just a nave and an aisle.

St Ethelburga survived the Great Fire of London, was restored in the Victorian era, and survived the First and Second World Wars, only to be nearly destroyed by an IRA bomb in 1993.

Following the bombing, proposals to sweep the church away and replace it with a modern office block were thwarted when the discovery that the south aisle and east window had survived, which led to a public outcry and demands that the whole church be rebuilt.

The church that stands in Bishopsgate today was rebuilt to resemble the original as much as possible.

St Ethelburga the Virgin is usually accepted as London's smallest church.

* * *

London's Smallest Listed Building

The ostler's hut in Lincoln's Inn.

Lincoln's Inn, to the south of Holborn, is the largest public square in London, known for its associations with the law and its practitioners. It was once said that the area was laid out to be exactly the same size as the base of the Great Pyramid of Giza, the oldest pyramid in Egypt. More recent accurate measurements, however, have shown this to be more fanciful than true. What is true, is that Lincoln's Inn contains what is reputed to be smallest listed building in London.

The Grade II building question is an ostler's hut. An ostler is an old name for a person whose job it was to look after the single horses of customers who rode them to, and stayed at, an inn, or those that were used to pull guests' carriages.

The hut in Lincoln's Inn was built in 1860 and its occupant looked after the horses of law students who worked in the area. Although described as a hut, it is actually a small red brick building with stone dressings and a wrought iron enclosed platform on the roof. The windows are square, and the doorway has a pointed arch above it.

The building fell into disuse when the role of the ostler died out with the coming of the motor car, which resulted in less reliance on horses for transport.

* * *

Soho's Half-Timbered House

Half-timbered houses in Britain date to the seventeenth century, when an abundance of oak made it the most common material for building. The term 'half-timbered' refers to the way the wooden logs were halved or cut square to be used as timbers in the construction of a building.

So the distinctive style, showing black wooden timbers with white infill, dates mostly from the Tudor period. The small house-like Tudor-style building in the middle of Soho Square, however, was built in 1925.

The gardener's hut in Soho Square isn't as old as it looks.

Originally, Soho Square was also known as King Square, after King Charles II, whose statue stood there from 1681. When the statue was removed in 1876, a small gardeners' hut was erected on this site, and a legend sprung up that it was actually the secret entrance to a tunnel that travelled under London to Buckingham Palace.

The half-timbered hut in the middle of Soho Square today was built in 1925, using original seventeenth-century wooden beams, to disguise an electricity substation belonging to the Charring Cross Electricity Company.

It was refurbished in 2009 and is now once again used as a storage place for the Square's gardeners.

* * *

Eisenhower's Command Base

During the Second World War, deep-level shelters were built at eight strategic stations on the London Underground. They could accommodate up to 8,000 people and were equipped with bunks, medical facilities, kitchens and bathrooms.

The entrance to one such shelter is situated at the junction of Chenies Street and North Crescent, close to Goodge Street station. It stands out amongst its neighbouring buildings because of its distinctive art deco design, and today is called the Eisenhower Centre.

The art deco building that was once Eisenhower's command base.

The reason it holds that prestigious name is because, during the Second World War, it served as General Dwight Eisenhower's command base at the time of the D-Day landings, the war's largest amphibious attack when the Allies invaded Western Europe on 6 June 1944.

* * *

The Winchester Palace Rose Window

Close to the path that runs along the south bank of the river Thames, in Clink Street at Southwark, lie the ruins of Winchester Palace, one of the few existing remains of medieval London.

Its name dates back to the thirteenth century, when the town of Southwark came under the Diocese of Winchester, the town in Hampshire that was capital of Saxon England. When the Bishop of Winchester decided to construct a palace for himself as a base in London, he had the building designed to incorporate a Great Hall and wine cellar, with a brewery, butcher's and even a prison in its grounds. It acted as a place of rest and entertainment, and played host to royal visitors for the next 500 years.

The rose window is the most prominent part of all that's left of Winchester Palace.

Destroyed by fire in the fifteenth century, the ruins were partially rediscovered in the nineteenth century, and more was found during redevelopment of the area in the 1980s. Today, the magnificent Rose Window in the west gable, comprising various sizes of hexagons, triangles and radiating daggers, all set in a circular design, marks what little remains of the Palace.

* * *

The Cathedral of Sewage

The year 1858 in London became known as the year of The Great Stink, due to the overwhelming smell of sewage dumped into the river Thames. As a result, a bill was rushed through Parliament to provide the money to construct an ambitious sewer system for London.

The new system had to take into account the fact that the river Thames was tidal. Therefore, anything discharged into the river in Central London might be washed downriver with the tide, but would surely return when the tide turned. To be effective, if waste were to be dumped in the river, it needed to be at a point closer to the Thames Estuary, and from there into the sea. The proposal was to intercept the sewage on its way to the river, and by means of both gravity and pumping stations along the way, divert it to two locations in the Thames Estuary.

Sir Joseph Bazalgette, the architect of London's sewage system, designed Abbey Mills Pumping Station in Abbey Lane, near Stratford

Stratford's aptly named Cathedral of Sewage.

in East London. It was built between 1865 and 1868. But if you expect an ugly subject like sewage to be in need of an ugly building, think again. This pumping station is an ornate Grade II listed Victorian building that looks like a cross between a royal palace and one of the great railway stations, with domed towers, arches over windows and doorways, delicate brickwork and ornate cast-iron decoration.

Soon after it was built, it earned the nickname The Cathedral of Sewage. In more recent times, the building has been used as a location for period dramas and the Batman films.

* * *

The Old Curiosity Shop

In 1841, Charles Dickens wrote his fourth novel, which also turned out to be his fourth best-seller. It was called *The Old Curiosity Shop* and told the tale of Little Nell and her gambling addict grandfather who fall into debt and are forced to flee their home in the antique and curio shop of the title.

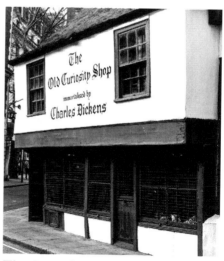

The sixteenth-century shop that claims to have inspired Dickens's novel.

Whether or not the shop in Portsmouth Street in London's Holborn really did inspire Dickens to write his novel is in some doubt, even though a sign emblazoned across the front proclaims that the shop was immortalised by the author. What isn't in doubt is that the shop was built in the sixteenth century, making it likely to be the oldest shop in Central London. It is also known that Charles Dickens lived in nearby Bloomsbury for a while and knew the location very well. It is more than likely that he visited the shop during his time in the area and it is perfectly plausible that the shop inspired his novel. It certainly fits the description of the building in his story.

The shop stands on land given by Charles II to one of his mistresses. It was built from wood that came from old sailing ships, and was once a dairy. Today it still functions as a working shop, though not the kind that sells curiosities.

* * *

The OXO Tower

What do you do when you own a company that produces a famous meat stock cube, but bylaws dictate that you're not allowed to advertise it on the front of your building? This is what happened when the Liebig Extract of Meat Company acquired an old power station on the south bank of the river Thames at Southwark in the 1920s.

As the power station was rebuilt for the meat company's use, the original intention was to include a tower with illuminated signs advertising the product. But when permission was refused on the grounds that skyline advertising was banned along the south bank of the river Thames, architect Albert Moore got round the problem in an ingenious way.

Subtle advertising on the OXO Tower.

On each of the four faces of a tower that topped the building he designed three vertically aligned windows. The top and bottom windows were built in the shape of an 'O', and the middle window was in the shape of an 'X'.

That's why today, the windows of the tower still standing above the building conveniently spell out the word 'OXO', the name of the meat extract cube invented by German chemist Justus von Liebig back in 1840. The word is particularly evident when the windows are lit up at night.

At the time it was built, the building was known as Stamford Wharf, where meat was delivered by barge to loading bays that can still be seen, into the building's cold stores, where it was processed and packed. In the 1920s, it was London's second highest commercial building.

Today, the building houses boutiques, studios, cafés and restaurants. The tower is not open to the public.

* * *

The Temple Church

Squeezed between Fleet Street and the river Thames in the City of London, there stands a strangely shaped circular church. It dates back to the twelfth century, when it was built by the Knights Templar, the leading powerful and wealthy Western Christian Military founded to protect pilgrims on their way to and from Jerusalem in the centuries before the Middle Ages. Temple Church was built as their English headquarters.

The circular part of the church is the oldest aspect of the building. It is known as the Round Church and

The original circular part of Temple Church.

acts as the knave, 55 feet in diameter and containing very early free-standing columns of Purbeck marble. The chancel is contained in a rectangular building that was added to the east side about fifty years after the original building was completed.

The church is open to the public most days, and is worth a visit if only to witness the incredible light that suffuses the interior from its windows, even on the cloudiest of days.

Recognised as one of the most historic and beautiful churches in London, it today stands adjacent to an area also known as The Temple, the famous centre for English law.

* * *

Canonbury Tower

Islington in North London is where you'll find Canonbury Tower, a tall, square building that seems to be squashed between two far more conventional houses. Over the years, it has been home to historical figures who have included philosopher and essayist Francis Bacon and playwright Oliver Goldsmith. Charles Dickens set one of his Christmas stories here as well.

The Tower is attached to an ancient manor house that dates back to 1509, which was later granted by Henry VIII to Thomas Cromwell for his help

Canonbury Tower, in Islington.

in the dissolution of the monasteries. In the 1590s, when the house was rebuilt by Lord Mayor of the City of London Sir John Spencer, he added the tower. It is one of the oldest buildings in Islington.

For fifty years, until 2003, the Tower was home to The Tower Theatre Company, London's most active amateur theatre group. Today, it is used as a Masonic research centre.

* * *

The Bells of Old Bond Street

On the corner of Old Bond Street and Burlington Gardens stands a shop that has been selling perfumes and beauty products on this spot since 1832. On its roof there is a spire, housing London's only carillon.

A carillon is a musical instrument whose sound is produced from bells played in harmony by an experienced carillonneur using a clavier, consisting of foot pedals and batons connected to the bells. The batons are struck with the player's fists.

This carillon was built in 1927 and is one of only fifteen in the whole of the UK. It was designed by Gillett and Johnston, a firm of clockmakers, established in 1844 and still in business today.

The carillon in Old Bond Street is played regularly, often on Friday evenings and Saturday afternoons, or on other special occasions.

* * *

Henry Moore Comes to Bond Street

The Time & Life building, named after the American news magazines of the same names, and which stands on the corner of New Bond Street and Bruton Street, is home to several high fashion shops. Three floors up, above one of the shops, it also boasts four stone sculptures by renowned English sculptor and artist Henry Moore.

Henry Moore sculptures on the roof of a New Bond Street building.

In 1951, Moore, who is famous for his abstract bronze sculptures seen as public art at numerous locations around the world, developed an interest in using his sculptures as part of the architectural design of buildings. That was when he accepted a commission from architect Michael Rosenauer, who was working on the design for the Time & Life Building.

The commission was to produce a screen that integrated with the design of the building, as part of the overall architecture. The screen would front a rooftop terrace, which made it more like a balustrade, with the space behind it allowing light to shine through the sculptures. Moore's original intention was to place the sculptures on rotating mounts to enable them to be turned to show different facets, but that idea was rejected for safety reasons.

He originally designed the sculptures as maquettes – small-scale drafts of the proposed sculptures – which were cast in bronze and sold as limited editions. The stone sculptures on the Time & Life Building were executed by sculptor Peter King, working from Moore's drawings. Moore was pleased with the result but expressed his disappointment that the sculptures could not be made to revolve and that they were positioned too high on the building to be readily appreciated by the passing public.

* * *

The Turkish Baths of Bishopgate

London is full of odd and ancient buildings that appear to have been dropped incongruously into the middle of far more modern developments. Such is the case with the Victorian Turkish Baths building to be found, surrounded by glass-fronted office blocks, in Bishopsgate.

The building, decorated in a Turkish style, is topped by an onion-shaped cupola with a star and crescent above. It was originally opened in 1895 as The New Broad Street Turkish Baths, a place for City gentlemen to relax. Inside, a winding earthenware tiled staircase originally led down to the baths, which were situated below street level.

In the 1970s, this area was extensively redeveloped, but the owners of the Turkish baths building held out against selling their little piece of Victorian London. In the end, the property developers built around the historic building, which is why it now stands strangely amid the modernity of the surrounding architecture.

The building's use as a Turkish bath ended long ago, since when it has been used by several restaurateurs and a night club owner, offering a unique place deep under the city to dine and party.

Bishopsgate's Turkish baths, surrounded by modern office blocks.

* * *

What's Left of the Euston Arch

Two of what must be the most compact public houses in London stand on either side of the entrance to Euston station on Euston Road. They are called the Euston Tap and the Cider Tap. Two storeys high and a mere 24 feet square, they were built in 1870 in the Grecian style with added Victorian ornamentation. They are all that is left of the Euston Arch, which once stood magnificently at the station entrance, filling the 80-foot gap between the tiny pubs.

The Euston Arch was inspired by Roman architecture and was designed

One of the two remaining Euston Lodges.

Euston Arch in the Victorian era.

by Phillip Hardwick, an architect particularly associated with railway stations. Although named as an arch, it was more of a gateway with huge Doric columns in the style of the entrance to the Acropolis in Athens.

The arch was demolished by hand over the course of several weeks in 1961, just leaving the twin lodges that once stood on either side. Golden gilded letters in the brickwork proclaim the destinations to which the railway ran from Euston station.

* * *

The Embassy of Texas

In St James Street, opposite the gates to St James's Palace, there is a narrow alleyway between two buildings. Halfway along there is a door with a plaque outside that announces: 'Texas Legation. In this building was the legation for the ministers from the Republic of Texas to the Court of St James 1842–1845.' Before it became a part of the United States in 1845, this is where the Republic of Texas housed its London Embassy.

The plaque outside the building that was once the Texas Embassy.

It dates back to a time when the Republic of Texas, fearing invasion from Mexico, set out to cultivate ties with other countries around the world. The country's London embassy – known then as a legation – was one of three, the others being located in Paris and Washington DC.

The London legation was actually the diplomatic address of Dr Ashbel Smith, who had been appointed as the Texan ambassador. The building was known as a notorious gambling den.

When Texas joined the United States, the legation was closed down. The plaque that stands outside the building today was instigated by the Anglo-Texan Society and put in place in 1963.

* * *

Where Taxi Drivers Take Shelter

At thirteen locations around London, often on pavements beside busy roads, you'll find small green buildings, looking rather like overgrown garden sheds. Nearby you're likely also to find a taxi rank. The two go together because these are the last remaining cabmen's shelters. They have been providing food, a place of rest and a shelter for drivers of

One of the few remaining cabmen's shelters, at Embankment Place.

hansom cabs and hackney carriages – otherwise known today as taxis – since 1875.

The shelters were set up by the Earl of Shaftsbury, who headed up a charity, founded in 1874, called the Cabmen's Shelter Fund. Since cabbies were traditionally not allowed to leave or move far from their vehicles when parked, the shelters were there to provide them with wholesome food at reasonable prices.

Originally, sixty-one shelters were built around London at a cost of about £200 each. Each contained a kitchen, tables and seating for about a dozen men. They were also full of newspapers and books, donated by their publishers and others. Gambling, drinking and swearing were strictly forbidden.

Those that have survived today are still used by taxi drivers. Some shelters also sell food and drink to the passing public, although only cabbies are allowed inside.

* * *

The Railway of the Dead

Westminster Bridge House at 121 Westminster Bridge Road is an ancient and ornate building sandwiched between two smaller office blocks. Its entrance at ground level is through a huge concrete archway. Above that, three storeys of windows are flanked by stone columns and topped by decorative porticoes with more curved ornamentation at roof level. It looks like the entrance to a Victorian railway station, which isn't surprising, because that's exactly what it was when it marked the entrance to the London Necropolis Railway.

Between the start and the middle of the nineteenth century, London's population

The terminus of the London Necropolis Railway.

quadrupled, whilst at the same time, more people than ever were dying from diseases that were rife in the City. London was running out of burial sites.

The solution came in the shape of a Brookwood Cemetery – the largest in the world at that time – which was opened 25 miles outside London in Surrey. The problem was how to get the bodies and mourners to the site. The answer to that came from Victorian entrepreneurs Sir Richard Broun and Richard Sprye, who not only built the cemetery, but also opened a special railway to covey coffins and mourners from the centre of London straight into the burial ground by means of a branch line of the London and South Western Railway, better known as the LSWR. They called it the London Necropolis Railway.

The original London terminus, opened in 1854, was close to Waterloo station. It housed private waiting rooms for mourners, places where funeral ceremonies could take place and hydraulic lifts to

The London Necropolis
Company.

ESTABLISHED 1850.

NEW   OFFICES
AND   PRIVATE   RAILWAY   STATION

121, Westminster Bridge Road.

CEMETERY:

BROOKWOOD, NR. WOKING.

The largest and most beautiful
in Great Britain.

Trade Discount on Fees, 5 per cent.

Registered Telegraphic Address : " Tenebratio, London."
Telephone No. 839 Hop.

How the London Necropolis Company advertised its services.

The Brookwood Cemetery Railway

End of the line at Brookwood Cemetery.

shift coffins to the level of the train platform. First, second and third class services were offered for live mourners and dead passengers like.

In 1902, when Waterloo station was expanded, the London Necropolis station was shifted to Westminster Bridge Road and the building was purposely designed to look as attractive as possible to contrast with more conventional funeral parlours.

In 1918, when the LSWR abolished second class travel for passengers on its trains, it forgot to extend that to the dead on the Necropolis Railway. Consequently, the dead passengers received first, second and third class services, while the live passengers had the option of only two classes.

The Necropolis Railway ran until 1941. Apart from the building, now housing offices, that remains today in Westminster Bridge Road, the only other present reminder of the London Necropolis Railway is a short section of railway track still remaining in Brookwood Cemetery.

* * *

Taking Their Toll

At each end of the Albert Bridge, which spans the river between Chelsea and Battersea, there is a strange, six-sided building with a door in one side and an overhanging roof. They have been there since 1873, when the bridge was first completed (a decade later, it proved structurally unsound and had to be redesigned) and today serve no useful purpose.

One of the two tollbooths that still remain on Albert Bridge.

The bridge was built at the instigation of Prince Albert, husband and Prince Consort of Queen Victoria, who thought it would help ease congestion on Victoria Bridge – now called Chelsea Bridge – and Battersea Bridge, which was in a poor state of repair. He also thought it would be a good idea to make it a toll bridge, and these two buildings were the original tollbooths.

The idea was not a great success, and in 1879, the Albert Bridge, along with others along this stretch of the river, was purchased by the Metropolitan Board of Works, who closed the booths and declared the bridge free to use.

The tolls only lasted six years, but the booths, used to collect the revenue, remain to this day.

* * *

The Guiltspur Street Watch House

At the edge of St Sepulchre's graveyard on Giltspur Street there stands a building known as a watch house. It is so called because this is the place where watchmen once stood guard over the graves to thwart body snatchers.

Body snatching reached epidemic proportions in the seventeenth century, when medical students would pay high prices for recently

The Watch House
that looks over
St Sepulchre's
graveyard.

deceased bodies that they needed for dissection and study. The bodies
of murderers were the only legal options for the purpose, so supply
and demand being what it was meant that grave robbing became a
highly lucrative business.

Naturally, students required newly dead bodies, rather than those
that had been interred for any length of time, so the watchmen in the
watch house were especially vigilant immediately after any funeral.

The bust in a small memorial on the side wall of the watch house is
of English essayist Charles Lamb, who, as a boy, attended services at
St Sepulchre's.

* * *

The Origin of Wedding Cakes

Traditionally, wedding cakes are made in tiers, each one slightly
smaller than the one below. The origins for this design are believed to
lie in the shape of the spire of St Bride's Church in Fleet Street.

St Bride's stands on a site of Christian Worship that dates back to
Roman times. The original church was destroyed by the Great Fire of
London in 1666, and was rebuilt under the direction of Christopher

Wren, the architect of St Paul's Cathedral. During the Second World War, in 1940, the church became a victim of the German air raids, with rebuilding not completed until the late 1950s.

The church's distinctive feature, which dates back to Wren's design, is its unusual spire, consisting of four structures, on top of each other, their sizes diminishing as they ascend, and crowned with a conical steeple.

Legend has it that, back in 1703, a baker's apprentice named Thomas Rich from nearby Ludgate Hill fell in love with his boss's daughter and asked her to marry him. Wanting to surprise his bride on her wedding day with an unusual cake, and being

The spire and steeple of St Bride's Church, said to have inspired traditional wedding cake designs.

a baker, he was in the ideal position to make it happen. He didn't have to look far for his inspiration, as the tiered levels of St Bride's Church spire inspired his cake design.

The cake was the first of its kind, but soon became popular, and remains so today.

* * *

The Cornhill Devils

High up at the top of a Victorian building situated at 54–55 Cornhill, three hideous devil-like statues gaze down ferociously at the church of St Peter upon Cornhill.

St Peter's is one of the oldest – some say *the* oldest – places of Christian worship in Britain. The church was yet another of those designed by Christopher Wren, following the Great Fire of London.

Today, the church is almost hidden behind blocks of offices that have surrounded it over the many years since it was built, and the building of which began in the late nineteenth century.

One story from this time concerns the way plans outlined by a developer stole land from St Peter's on which to build an office block. When challenged by one of the church's vicars, the office block architect was forced to withdraw his plans and go right back to the drawing board, something that cost him dearly. As

The Cornhill devils.

revenge, when the newly designed building was completed, he added three terracotta devil-like figures, each with a fiendish expression and threatening pose. Today, all three still glare down at the entrance to St Peter's from the upper levels of the newer building.

It is said that the devil nearest to the church bears the face of the vicar who caused the architect so much time, trouble and expense.

Chapter 4

What Happened to the Festival Exhibition

In 1951, a national event officially known as The Festival of Britain: A Land and its People was launched. Its purpose was to celebrate Britain's recovery, following the end of the Second World War six years before. The event was national, but its centrepiece was The South Bank Exhibition in London, based at Lambeth on the south bank of the river Thames, between Waterloo and Westminster bridges.

Old Victorian buildings and railway sidings were demolished and new structures were built here incorporating exhibitions that explored Britain's landscape, people, industry and science. The most impressive of these was the Dome of Discovery, which at the time was the largest dome in the world. Inside, galleries on different levels showed displays of the living world, the physical world, the earth, the land, the sea, the sky and outer space. It was surrounded by many other smaller, but no less significant and fascinating exhibits.

King George VI opened the exhibition on 3 May 1951 and it closed on 30 September the same year. Almost immediately, work began on its demolition. By October, only a few weeks after the exhibition closed, the Conservatives returned to power with Winston Churchill as Prime Minister. The incoming government saw the Festival Exhibition as part of the misguided ideals of the previous Labour government, and viewed it, not as the successful event it turned out to be, but more as a symbol of financial mismanagement. For them, it became politically important to sweep away all traces of the exhibition as soon as possible.

Very little of the amazing Festival Exhibition remains today, but there are still traces to be found, in particular along the banks of the river Thames, if you know where to look for them.

* * *

Above: the Skylon and Dome of Discovery. Below: the Royal Festival Hall, Skylon and Dome of Discovery seen across the Thames at night.

The Royal Festival Hall

Many London curiosities are hidden away in unexpected places. The only real survivor of the Festival Exhibition is not among them. It's one of the most prominent buildings on the South Bank, which is why it's easy to overlook the important part it played in the 1951 Exhibition. In fact, it was the only aspect of the exhibition that was planned from the start to remain after the festivities were over. Here's what the Festival of Britain's South Bank Exhibition brochure said about the Royal Festival Hall in 1951.

The simplicity of the external design of the hall may give little hint of the care and skill which have gone into every detail of its construction. This has resulted not only in good acoustics, but also in the greatest comfort for audience and players. Innovations include the double-skinned wall, designed to exclude noise, and the tuning of the concert hall auditorium after the building work had been completed. The concert hall holds an audience of 3,300. There is also provision for an orchestra of more than 100 and a choir of 250.

In addition, the Royal Festival Hall can claim to be a work of art in itself. The superb dramatic effects of space and vista, within the building and beyond it to the river and the city, are things which the visitor will discover for himself.

The Royal Festival Hall is the most prominent reminder of the exhibition today.

Following various refurbishments of the hall since it opened with the exhibition in 1951, little has dramatically changed inside or out. Today it is a Grade I listed building, which stands at the heart of the South Bank Centre arts complex. It is free to visit, whether you are attending a concert or not, and is known for the excellence of its bars, restaurants, shops and riverside terrace café.

* * *

The Lion Brewery Lion

On the south bank of the river Thames outside County Hall (once the home of London County Council and now a luxury apartment development) stands the statue of a white lion. It appears to be made from concrete, but in fact is made from a composite called Coade's artificial stone, a kind of ceramic stoneware that was patented in 1722 and of which the exact composition has never been revealed.

The Lion Brewery lion in its current resting place at the end of Westminster Bridge.

The lion, which was cast in 1837, once stood on a parapet above Lion's Brewery in Lambeth, but was removed in 1949 when the building was demolished to make way for the South Bank Exhibition. When the building was torn down, the lion was moved, according to the wishes of King George VI, to York Road and erected outside Waterloo station, becoming part of the exhibition, whose site it overlooked. During this time, it was painted red. The statue remained there until 1966, long after the exhibition closed, when the paint was removed to reveal the white ceramic surface beneath, and it was once again moved, this time to its current position on Westminster Bridge.

The statue is 13 feet long, 12 feet high and weighs about 14 tons. Over the years, Coade's artificial stone has proved to be more durable than concrete and has stayed cleaner for longer, as is evidenced by the statue's cleanliness and the fine detailing of the creature's face, which has survived London's corrosive atmosphere until now, nearly 200 years after it was made.

* * *

The Regatta Restaurant

There were thirteen restaurants, cafés, bars and buffets on the exhibition site, the best of which was probably the Regatta Restaurant, situated to the west of the Royal Festival Hall, beneath and adjacent to Hungerford Bridge.

The restaurant catered for 500 people, serving lunch, tea, dinner and supper. The unusual decorative pattern of the furnishings and tableware was derived from diagrams made by scientists who mapped the arrangement of atoms in crystals studied by X-rays. This branch of science, known as X-ray crystallography, was particularly well developed in Britain at this time.

Entrance to the restaurant was via arched doorways at the river side of the building and at the opposite end, fronting what is now Belvedere Road. The arches were bricked up long ago, but their outlines can still be seen in a wall beneath Hungerford Bridge.

Hidden away under Hungerford Bridge, behind a line of rubbish bins, are the bricked-up arches to what was once the Festival's Regatta Restaurant.

Back in 1951, other examples of the crystallography patterns could also be seen in the Dome of Discovery and the Exhibition of Science in South Kensington.

* * *

Scrapping the Skylon

Sharing equal status with the Dome of Discovery as a major symbol of the South Bank Exhibition, the Skylon was a tall and extremely slender structure comprising a steel latticework frame, pointed at each end, bulging slightly in the middle and supported on cables slung between three steel struts. The effect was to make it look as though it was floating above the ground. *The Illustrated London News*, in its special festival issue of 12 May 1951, described it like this:

A beacon of light piercing upwards into the sky beckons visitors from far and near to the great Festival of Britain Exhibition on the South Bank of the Thames. This beacon is illuminated internally by a series of lamps grouped in clusters of three at frequent intervals round a central steel tube. Burnished aluminium cones reflect the light on to external reflectors. How very different will be the London scene by night this Festival summer when compared to the long nights of darkness that have preceded it.

How many dining in the Skylon Restaurant today know the importance of its name, or that the artwork on its sign shows what this amazing structure actually looked like?

The Skylon was dismantled in April 1952 and sold for scrap, an ignoble ending for an icon that so much symbolised the spirit of the exhibition. So there is nothing left of the amazing Skylon. There is, however, a small plaque on the South Bank to commemorate it.

The sign on the flagpole that commemorates the exhibition.

Remembering the Skylon with a plaque in the pavement of the South Bank.

Walk along the South Bank from Hungerford Bridge towards Westminster Bridge, and halfway between the two, you'll find a wooden flagpole that was originally erected at the exhibition. In a band that encircles it, is an inscription that explains:

> This flagpole, provided by the forest industry of British Columbia for the 1951 Festival of Britain, was re-erected by the Provincial Government of British Columbia in 1977 to mark the Silver Jubilee of Her Majesty Queen Elizabeth II.

Look on the ground beside the flagpole and you'll find a small circular plaque set flush with the pavement. At the top of the circle an inscription reads: 'Remembering the Skylon. Festival of Britain, 1951.' Around its circumference are the words: 'I saw a blade which rises in the sky held by hardly nothing at all.'

The Skylon also lives on as the name of a restaurant attached to the third floor of the Royal Festival Hall, with a style that echoes the 1950s and where modern British cuisine is on daily offer.

* * *

Finding the Festival Emblem

The Festival emblem, on the front cover of an original exhibition catalogue.

The Festival of Britain had a very distinctive emblem. It was designed by Abram Games, an official war poster artist who was demobbed in 1946, and who was one of twelve artists invited to submit designs to the Arts Council and the Council for Industrial Design in 1948. The emblem depicted the head of Britannia wearing a crested helmet at the top of a compass-like star, with festive bunting hanging in a semi-circle from the left and right points of the star and incorporating the year 1951.

The three plaques high on the façade of the building at 219 Oxford Street.

The whole thing was designed in the traditional red, white and blue of the Union Flag.

At one time, the emblem could often be seen incorporated into the names of streets or signs for areas of London that had connections with the exhibition. Today, few of these remain, but there is one building in Oxford Street that still exhibits the emblem and other symbols of the event.

High up on the facade of an office block at 219 Oxford Street, you can still see three plaques that refer to the exhibition. The building's shop and offices above were probably the first commercial premises to be erected in London after the Second World War. Most of the remains of the exhibition had been cleared away by the time the building was finished, but it would seem that the designers wanted to make some kind of acknowledgement of the spirit of new beginnings that informed the age, and so the three plaques were incorporated into the design.

Standing vertically adjacent to the top three floors of the building, the middle plaque shows the exhibition emblem. Above that, the top plaque shows the Dome of Discovery, the Skylon and navigational equipment. The lower one shows a crown, the Royal Festival Hall, an old shot tower that was incorporated into the exhibition and various musical instruments.

No other building in London still shows such clear references to the Festival of Britain.

* * *

Remembering Sherlock Holmes

Not every aspect of the Festival of Britain was centred on the South Bank Exhibition. Events took place all over the country, although there is scant evidence of most of them now. One aspect of the Festival that can still be seen in London, however, is located on the upstairs floor of a pub in Northumberland Street.

In 1951, 221B Baker Street, purported to be the home of the fictional detective Sherlock Holmes, was occupied by the Abbey

The Sherlock Holmes pub, in Northumberland Avenue.

National Building Society. Together with Marylebone Public Library, the support of author Arthur Conan Doyle's family and the help of a few volunteers, and as part of the Festival Exhibition, a display was mounted in Abbey House, the building society's Baker Street headquarters, to celebrate the fictional life of Sherlock Holmes.

The exhibit recreated Holmes's gaslit sitting room, with pictures, a blackboard, scientific apparatus, books and even fresh crumpets, complete with tooth marks, supplied each day by a local baker. Following the Festival of Britain, the exhibit toured the world.

The Sherlock Holmes exhibit that has survived from the Festival of Britain.

In 1957, the Northumberland Arms was refurbished and renamed The Sherlock Holmes. Then, following its world tour, the pub's owners acquired the entire Sherlock Holmes exhibit. Today, the detective's supposed sitting room can be seen behind a glass panel, viewed from the pub's first-floor restaurant and roof garden.

Chapter 5

On the Pineapple Trail

In 1493, a year after the start of his historic voyage that led to the opening up of the Americas to European travellers and explorers, Christopher Columbus returned from Guadeloupe bearing a strange fruit, the like of which no one in Europe had seen before: tough and scaly on the outside, but sweet and succulent on the inside. It was a pineapple, and in the centuries that followed, these rare delicacies became symbols of a person's affluence and hospitality. They also took on the role of good luck charms.

It was said that a sailor returning from the sea would place a pineapple outside his house as a sign that he was home safe and well. Soon, pineapples began to be incorporated into all kinds of architectural design, and today, many different forms and styles of the fruit can be seen on and around buildings all over London.

* * *

Lambeth Bridge

Lambeth Bridge crosses the river Thames between Westminster and Vauxhall Bridges. At each end there is a pair of obelisks topped with pineapples. There are conflicting opinions about why they are there and the most likely

Pineapples on obelisks at each side of Lambeth Bridge.

explanation is that they are simply a form of ornamentation, implemented by the architect as a sign of hospitality.

There is, however, a much more interesting urban myth about the pineapples, which are linked to a seventeenth-century botanist named John Tradescant, who is reputed to have introduced the pineapple to Britain. He is buried in what was once the graveyard of St Mary-in-Lambeth, situated at the eastern approach to the bridge. The deconsecrated church is now home to the Museum of Garden History.

* * *

St. Paul's Cathedral

St Paul's Cathedral sits at the top of Ludgate Hill, one of the highest points in London. It was designed by Sir Christopher Wren and the present building is at least the fourth to have stood at this location, having been built between 1675 and 1710, following the destruction of its predecessor in the Great Fire of London.

A pineapple tops one of the towers of St Paul's Cathedral.

Go to the western side, look up at the twin towers that so define the cathedral's design, and at the tops, where you might expect to find crosses, you'll actually see two golden pineapples.

It would seem that Wren was fond of using emblems of the fruit in his designs. Round the corner to St Paul's, in Newgate Street, there are the remains of Christ Church, one of the many other London churches also designed by the prolific architect. The building was bombed during the Second World War, but the stone pineapples that once adorned it remain in places, some of them having been seemingly discarded on the ground.

* * *

Stone pineapples in the remains of Christ Church in Newgate Street.

St. Pancras' Old Churchyard

Neo-classical architect Sir John Soane was buried in the churchyard of St Pancras Old Church, believed to be one of the oldest sites of Christian worship in London. But more than twenty years before his

The tomb of Sir John Soane, in St Pancras Old Churchyard.

death he designed his own mausoleum, in which his wife was interred following her death in 1815, and where he was also entombed in 1837.

Today, the tomb is Grade I listed, with a design that echoes the architectural design of many of Soane's buildings. A marble canopy is supported on four columns with a cube inside on which the usual inscriptions are placed, and a stairway leads down to the tomb. On the top of the canopy, there is a pineapple.

Many people who have seen the tomb feel it reminds them of something they can't quite place. The answer to that riddle is that the tomb's design was a strong influence on English architect Sir Giles Gilbert Scott, who, among other architectural triumphs, designed Britain's first red telephone box, very much in the style of Soane's tomb.

One of the remaining K2 telephone boxes, whose design is influenced by Sir John Soane's tomb. This one is in St John's Wood High Street.

Known as the K2, the telephone box was Scott's winning entry in a competition to find an appropriate design for a national telephone kiosk. It was introduced in 1926, and before a decade had passed, about 1,700 had been installed, mostly in London. Today, those that remain are Grade II listed. Needless to say, the telephone boxes do not have pineapples on their tops!

* * *

Street Furniture

Once you become conscious of the pineapple motif, you'll see it everywhere: as the finishing touches to roof decorations, often topping domes, on buildings that range from pubs to the National Gallery; and in particular, on railings that front houses.

Pineapples on railings, gateways and other entrances are particularly prevalent in front of the houses in Devonshire Street and nearby roads like Portland Place, some painted black, others bright gold.

Look carefully and you'll see them in stone, in iron, in plaster, sometimes huge and marking the entrance to an important building, other times small and hidden away on something as insignificant as a boot scraper outside the front door of a house.

Pineapples proliferate on the railings of houses in Devonshire Street.

You'll find them too at the top of lamp posts, especially many of the old gas lamps still found in the more ancient parts of London. Sometimes they stand alone, other times they are built into the stonework of a building. But nearly always, they are at entrances to residences, reinforcing their connections with both hospitality and affluence.

Once you start looking for London pineapples, you'll start to see them everywhere.

Pineapples on the rooftops of buildings in Piccadilly Circus.

Chapter 6

Windmills and Lighthouses

Windmills are situated in the windy countryside and lighthouses are built on, or some way off, the coast. That, generally, is the perceived wisdom. You'd expect to see neither in the urban landscape of London … unless, of course, you know where to look.

* * *

Brixton Windmill

Strange as it might seem today, windmills were a common sight in pre-industrial London. The Brixton Mill, in Windmill Gardens, not far from Brixton Prison, is one of the very few still remaining. It dates back to the nineteenth century, when this area was mostly agricultural land, more like the neighbouring county of Surrey than the accepted vision of South London.

John Muggeridge and Sons, a firm of builders already heavily involved in the development of Brixton, built the windmill in 1816. Officially known as Ashby's Mill, it was operated by William Ashby, a millwright from Kent. Nearby

Brixton Windmill, in South London.

was a large double-fronted Georgian villa called Mill House, where the Ashby family lived. Gardens, orchards and allotments surrounded the mill.

The mill worked by traditional wind-driven sails until 1862, when the milling business was shifted to a watermill at Mitcham. The sails were removed and the mill fell into disuse until 1902, when a steam engine was installed and business began again, using the mill to supply flour to London hotels and restaurants. With the later installation of a gas engine, the mill continued to work until 1934.

Narrowly escaping demolition after the Second World War, when it was suggested the site should be used to build a block of flats, Brixton Mill survived and is now open to the public for guided tours and educational visits.

* * *

The Wimbledon Windmill

Wimbledon is known for being the home of British lawn tennis and its world-renowned annual tournament. Second only to tennis, this South London suburb is famous for its common, not exactly a park, more an area of natural open land comprising woodland, streams, heath and ponds. The windmill, situated on the Common, is less well known.

In the eighteenth century, there were numerous steam-powered mills in and around this area. Many of these were owned by businessman John Watney, who understood that local residents had a need for their

The windmill on Wimbledon Common.

own mill, rather than relying on factories for their flour. In 1799, Watney applied to enclose a piece of land on Wimbledon Common, where he intended to erect a windmill.

Unfortunately, he died before his mill was built, but in 1816, carpenter Charles March from nearby Roehampton made a new application and was granted a 99-year lease for a yearly rent of two shillings (10p in today's decimal currency). The lease stated that it was granted 'upon this special condition that he shall erect and keep up a public Corn Mill for the advantage and convenience of the neighbourhood'.

The mill was built with an octagonal brick base with a wooden structure above it to house the milling machinery. A conical tower above this supported the cap on which the sails were mounted.

The mill worked until 1864, and a few years later it was converted to become living accommodation for six families. Today it is a working museum on the ground and first floor, with exhibits that explain the development and construction of windmills in general, as well as details of how this particular mill worked to mill grain and produce flour.

* * *

Barnet Gate Mill

The London Borough of Barnet was once part of Hertfordshire. Back in the days when this now urbanised area was mostly open countryside, it made a prime spot for a windmill, which still stands there today.

The mill is on private land off Brickfield Lane. It is known as both the Barnet Gate Mill and the Arkley Mill. Erected in 1826, it was worked by wind until 1895, when a steam engine was added. Subsequently it worked by both steam and wind power, until 1918.

The mill was designed as a four-storey tower mill, consisting of a brick tower with the sails attached to a domed cap, which rotated according to wind direction. It was originally built for grinding corn.

* * *

London's Only Lighthouse

London has several lighthouse-type structures and buildings, but the one at Trinity Buoy Wharf deep in the heart of the London Docklands, where the river Thames meets the river Lee, is London's only genuinely authentic example.

London's only true lighthouse, in Docklands.

For nearly 200 years, the Corporation of Trinity House, which has been looking after the safety of shipping and seafarers since being granted a Royal Charter by Henry VIII in 1514, used this area as a lightship dock, for buoy storage and as a maintenance depot. It was also a place where lighthouse technology and new types of lamp were once tested. For that purpose, London's only true lighthouse was built here between 1864 and 1866.

Michael Faraday, the eminent English scientist, whose fields of interest were in electromagnetism and electrochemistry, performed his experiments here, and also in another smaller lighthouse that was built nearby in 1854, but demolished in the 1920s.

The Wharf closed in the late 1980s, but in 1996 a private company leased the site and developed it as a cultural centre, where you can now see oddities ranging from an office and studio block made from recycled shipping containers, to a lightship that has been transformed into a photographic studio, as well as a full-size replica of an American diner.

The Bow Creek Lighthouse, to give it its correct name, is open to the public and offers wonderful views of the river from the top. The eerie music that you might hear inside the building is called *Longplayer*. Thanks to modern technology and the work of a group of ingenious musicians, it was composed and designed to play for 1,000 years, beginning on 1 January 2000. Providing nothing goes wrong, it is hoped that the music will continue playing until 31 December 2999.

* * *

The King's Cross Lighthouse

Walk out of King's Cross station in North London, look to the left and raise your eyes to rooftop level and you'll see what appears to be a lighthouse protruding from the top of a Victorian building sandwiched between the meeting point of Pentonville Road and Gray's Inn Road. It certainly looks like a lighthouse, but it's doubtful that it was designed as such. So what is it and why was it placed here on this rooftop?

One clue might be that, back in Victorian times, the building served as an oyster house, and one popular seller, namely Netten's Oyster House, which operated from the ground floor, used a lighthouse as a symbol or trademark.

The roof of a Victorian building is the unlikely location for a lighthouse at King's Cross.

Maybe it was an early form of advertising where this popular fast food of the day could be bought.

Other theories as to its origins and the reason for its design are regularly put forward, and then just as regularly dismissed. It has been suggested that it might have been a clock tower, a windmill, a camera obscura and even a Victorian helter-skelter that someone decided to hoist up onto the roof. The truth is that it is little more than a folly, and no one seems to know how it got there, or why it was made to resemble a lighthouse.

Until such time as the truth comes to light, the King's Cross Lighthouse will remain a charming and intriguing curiosity.

* * *

The Walthamstow Methodist Lighthouse

The Lighthouse Methodist Church in Walthamstow, East London, is well named. After all, it has a lighthouse on its roof.

Its origins date back to 1887, when a group of young people from the Wesleyan Church, a few miles away, split to set up their own church in a nearby house. When its success meant that larger premises were needed, a piece of land was bought by one of the church's supporters, a Captain King of Bullard King Steamers, which ran a service from London to East Africa. Later, in

Lighthouse Methodist Church, in Walthamstow.

1892, he paid for the present building to be erected on the site. It became the best attended nonconformist church in Walthamstow, with congregations, by the early 1900s, in excess of 1,500.

As a reminder of his seafaring activities, Captain King requested that the design should incorporate a lighthouse on its roof. In its early days, a revolving light shone out from the top of the lighthouse to call the congregation to prayer, in much the same way as bells in a traditional church bell tower were used for a similar purpose. The light would continue to revolve, reminiscent of a real lighthouse, while the service was taking place.

Today, a light still remains lit right at the top of the lighthouse during some Sunday services.

Chapter 7

Curious Clocks

Clocks have always held a fascination for designers and artists, many of whom have been unable to resist going overboard with their creative eccentricities. London abounds with them.

* * *

The Largest Clock in London

At number 80 Strand (more popularly known as The Strand) there stands an office block, designed in the art deco style and built in 1930, originally as the headquarters for Shell-Mex and BP Ltd.

When it was built, height restrictions were in place for London buildings, which prevented it being built any higher than twelve floors that reached 190 feet. There was, however, a loophole. The restrictions

The largest clock in London, seen from Hungerford Bridge.

applied to the inhabited parts of a building. There was nothing to stop the designers and builders adding to the height with an uninhabited section. So they added a clock. It was – and still is – the largest clock in London.

Seen from ground level, the clock doesn't look as impressive as you might expect. The best view of the building and the clock, from which you get a far better sense of its size, is from the eastern walkway of Hungerford Bridge. The two clock faces, which can be seen from the road side and the river side, are each 25 feet in diameter.

After the Second World War, when height restrictions were revoked, an extra two storeys of office space were added to the building.

* * *

Where Mr Fortnum Meets Mr Mason

Fortnum and Mason, in Piccadilly, is one of the most famous stores in London. It dates back to 1707, when William Fortnum was a footman in the royal household. The Royal Family insisted on having new candles at dinner every night, and Fortnum's job was to replace them

Each hour, and on the hour, Mr Fortnum and Mr Mason emerge from the closed doors either side of the clock.

at the end of each day, even if only a small amount of wax had been used. Being a bit of an entrepreneur, he sold the used candles for a profit.

Fortnum's landlord was Hugh Mason and together they set up a small shop in Piccadilly, with Fortnum's wax selling profits contributing to the cash required for their enterprise. The shop immediately prospered, thanks in no small part to Fortnum's royal connections, which he used to get business.

From these humble beginnings, the great store in Piccadilly grew and flourished, retaining its royal connections throughout the Victorian age and onwards to today, when the store is often referred to as the Royal Grocer.

In 1964, it was decided to build the huge and very ornate clock that now stands above the main entrance to the building. Because it's between two windows on the second storey and some way above eye level, it's easy to miss it, and even when you see it, you won't understand what's so special about it unless you are there at the top of the hour.

The clock features a large, highly decorative round face between two equally decorative towers with two doors in each. When the clock chimes, it does so courtesy of eighteen bells. But the best part happens every hour, on the hour. As the chimes begin, the doors in the towers open inwards and two 4-foot automatons of Mr Fortnum and Mr Mason emerge, one holding a tea service on a tray, the other holding a candelabra, to meet in front of the clock, where they turn their heads and bow to each other. Then, having ascertained that all is well with their great store, they turn, move back inside, and the doors close behind them.

* * *

The Queen of Time

It seems that great department stores often demand great timepieces above their entrances. Selfridges in Oxford Street is no exception. A dynamic American named Harry Gordon Selfridge opened the store in 1906. He was a man who, more than most of his time, understood the importance of how publicity, promotion and sheer theatricality could do so much for retail selling.

The Queen of Time, above the main entrance to Selfridges.

It's a tradition that remains today and is nicely summed up by the clock that stands above the store's main entrance. It was the work of sculptor Gilbert Bayes, who was particularly interested in the use of colour in decorative sculpture. The Selfridges clock is perhaps his most famous work; it was produced in 1908 and named The Queen of Time.

Below the two-faced clock, the Queen is a larger than life-size sculpture that stands on the prow of a ship, with waves and art deco-style mermaids on each side. She holds an orb topped by a small winged figure in her right hand and a bunch of leaves is clasped above her head in her left hand. Another ship stands at the top of the clock. Two more winged youths and a couple of semi-nude female figures also adorn and flank the central Queen figure. The clock chimes on the hour and every quarter.

* * *

Greenwich's 24-Hour Clock and Time Ball

On a wall beside the gates to the Observatory in the Greater London Borough of Greenwich there is a strange clock with the usual two hands but with a twenty-four hour face, whose hours are designated by Roman numerals from 0 at the twelve o'clock position to XXIII at the usual eleven o'clock position.

The twenty-four-hour clock outside Greenwich Observatory.

One of the Observatory's claims to fame is for being the home of Greenwich Mean Time, the place where each new day, year and millennium officially starts at the stroke of midnight. Its genesis lay in the growing network of railways that spread across England in the Victorian era. At this time, it was rare for many people to own a clock or a watch, and most relied on public sundials to tell the time. That led to different local times across Britain, with sundials in the east of the country being anything up to thirty minutes ahead of those in the west. But if railways were to run effectively, they needed timetables, and timetables needed a single standard time to be used throughout the country.

Astronomer Royal George Airy was the man who suggested that this standard time should originate and emanate from the Royal Observatory. His idea was that a master clock would be based in Greenwich, from where it would transmit signals via electric telegraph to slave clocks right across Britain. The man tasked with the job of making all this happen was engineer Charles Shepherd, who had already patented such an idea and shown that it could work.

Shepherd's first task was to build one automatic clock to be housed within the Observatory, and from which signals would be transmitted to a large clock face at the Observatory entrance, where it could be seen by the public. The clock that is attached to the wall by the gates today is a replica of that first clock.

Signals from Shepherd's original master clock, as well as being sent to the clock at the gate, were also transmitted by cable to the London Bridge terminus of the South-Eastern Railway, from where they were sent along all the main railways routes that ran out from London, to a network of slave clocks throughout England.

Another strange time-related device can be seen on the roof of the Observatory. It's called a time ball, a device more traditionally located on buildings close to the coast and used by offshore sailors. They consisted of metal or wooden balls that were dropped down the length of a pole at predetermined and accurate times. The example on the Observatory's roof also received signals from Shepherd's

The time ball on the roof of the Observatory.

master clock, so that its decent ended precisely at 1.00 pm.

It still happens today. Be outside the gates at 1.00 pm, glance up at the roof of the Observatory, and you'll see the ball climbing to the top of its pole, then dropping back to the bottom dead on the appointed hour.

* * *

Switzerland Comes to London

In 1968, an unusual building was erected in Leicester Square to showcase Swiss culture and to encourage Londoners to visit Switzerland. It was called, unsurprisingly, The Swiss Centre. On the outside of the building there was a clock that featured moving figures in traditional Swiss costumes, who moved around to the accompaniment of ringing bells. In 2008, The Swiss Centre was demolished to make way for a large hotel, and the clock disappeared.

In 2011, the clock was restored and returned to Leicester Square in an area named Swiss Court, as a token of the lasting friendship between Switzerland and the United Kingdom. The clock is free-standing, more than 30 feet high and incorporates a glockenspiel. At regular times during the day, the bells play music as a procession of miniature Swiss herdsmen drive their animals up the hill of an alpine meadow.

Nearby, a Cantonal Tree displays the coats of arms of the twenty-six cantons (administrative divisions) of Switzerland.

The Swiss clock, in Leicester Square.

* * *

The twenty-six cantons of Switzerland displayed on the Cantonal Tree.

The Churchill Clock

Close to St Paul's Cathedral, Bracken House is a fairly unimposing building but one with an extremely striking entrance, above which stands a most unusual astronomical clock. At its centre, it incorporates the face of former British Prime Minister Sir Winston Churchill.

Bracken House was built to house the *Financial Times* newspaper and its printing works. It was named after Brendan Bracken, who was best known for merging the *Financial*

Sir Winston Churchill gazes out from the centre of the Bracken House clock.

News with the *Financial Times* in 1945, thereby creating probably the best-respected financial newspaper in Britain.

The building was designed and built in pink sandstone to match the colour of the newspaper.

Among his other many business and political accomplishments, Bracken served in Churchill's wartime government as Minister of Information, before returning to the publishing business at the end of the war. The two men became firm friends and when Bracken had the clock installed in 1955, he arranged for it to incorporate the face of Churchill as a tribute to his friend and mentor.

There are no hands, but instead, the various dials rotate anticlockwise around Churchill's face to display the current time in hours and minutes, the month of the year, phase of the moon and sign of the zodiac.

* * *

Aquatic Horology

In Covent Garden on the wall above a shop at 21–23 Shorts Gardens, there is a clock that once worked by water. It was created in 1982 by two artists, Tim Hunkin and Andy Plant, who called themselves aquatic horologists.

The clock, which has a green face, is suspended halfway up a ladder, at the base of which a row of figures stands ready with watering cans. Below the clock face, a tube slowly fills with water, its rise indicating minutes. Then, on the hour, water is tipped from a tank on the roof of the building to run down the side, activating a series of bells above the clock face. At the same time, the figures below tip their watering cans to fill a tank behind the shop sign in which plastic flowers float. As the tank is filled, the

The aquatic clock, in Covent Garden.

flowers rise to give the impression that they are growing.

The clock no longer operates, but might yet be restored. Even in its non-working condition, it still stands as an interesting curiosity. When the clock was working, it was not a good idea to stand beneath the figure on the left of the row. This one was designed to swing out and pour the contents of its watering can over the heads of anyone below.

* * *

Strictly for the Birds

Outside the tropical aviary at London Zoo in Regents Park there is strange clock featuring a host of automaton birds. Like the aquatic clock in Covent Garden, this one was also designed by artist Tim Hunkin.

When the artist was first commissioned in 2008, his brief was to design a feature that would sum up the Victorians' attitude to the animal kingdom. With his love of clocks, Hunkin soon realised that was the way his design would go. His first thought was to place a clock in a cage, but he was told that cages were somewhat frowned upon by zoos these days. So he switched his attention to thoughts about birds escaping. This became the unifying strand in the clock's design.

Tim Hunkin's bird-themed clock in London Zoo.

The clock stands on a plinth, below which are figures holding a meat pan and cage, birds in a display case and two toucans each side of the pendulum. Above the clock is a revolving arm with more birds strung below it on wires.

At the top of each hour, here's what happens. The toucans at the base of the clock peck at the pendulum to keep it moving. The figure on the left holding the meat pan lifts the lid to reveal a trembling bird beneath. The cage held by the figure on the right opens and a bluebird escapes. More small birds escape from the display case. The figure on the left closes the lid on the meat pan, and then lifts it again to reveal that the bird has gone. The arm above the clock revolves with the birds flying beneath it. The toucans disappear from beneath the clock and reappear, squawking, above it. Without their help, the pendulum stops swinging. Everything stops and the whole sequence is repeated an hour later.

* * *

Last of the London Bridge Dairy Farm

Just over London Bridge, at the top of a wall at the point where Borough High Street meets the entrance to London Bridge station, there is a clock under a stone arch. Rather incongruously, the head of a cow, complete with horns, protrudes from the wall above the clock face.

It would seem to be a strange symbol to place on a clock in an area that's so thoroughly urbanised today. But go back in time and this site was occupied by a large dairy, through which farmers from Kent brought milk and dairy produce to London.

Today, a small stone cow's head is all that remains of this ancient enterprise.

The cow above the clock that reminds Londoners of the dairy that once stood here.

* * *

Southwark's Black Face Clock

The church of St George the Martyr in Southwark, South London, has a clock tower with four faces looking north, south, east and west. Three of the clock faces are white, but the one facing east is black. A number of reasons for this have been put forward over the years, but the most popular goes like this.

Back in 1734, when the church was being rebuilt, an appeal went out for those living in the surrounding areas to make financial contributions towards the work. It's reckoned that the people to the north, south and west of the church came up with the

The black clock face and one of the three white faces on the tower of St George the Martyr in Southwark.

requested cash, but those who lived in Bermondsey, to the east, failed to deliver. Several reasons were offered: they were too poor, too mean or just plain rebellious.

Whatever the reason, the church authorities decided that if the people of Bermondsey were not prepared to contribute to the church, then the church would deny them the opportunity of seeing the time. So the eastern side of the clock tower was left blank. A little later, it seems, there was a change of heart and a clock was installed, but as a reproach to the people who had failed to help rebuild the church, this one face was coloured black, rather than the white of the other three faces.

* * *

The Caledonian Clock Tower

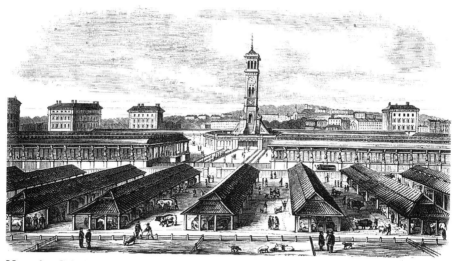

How the Caledonian Clock Tower looked in 1855, when there was a cattle market here.

Sometimes architects and designers go to extraordinary lengths to house a public clock. That's certainly the case with the clock tower in Caledonian Park, just off Market Street, Islington.

The site was once known as Copenhagen Fields, a popular place for demonstrations. In 1855, it became the Metropolitan Cattle Market, which was opened by Prince Albert. Covering 30 acres, it was dominated by the clock tower. With the market long gone, the same tower now stands in the park, which covers 18 acres. It is said that the Tower was built to withstand a bull stampede.

The Tower stands seven storeys high and features a clock face said to have been originally designed for Big Ben, the name by which the clock tower that

The Caledonian Clock Tower today.

stands at one end of the Houses of Parliament is popularly known. A public gallery surrounds the tower above the clock face.

Following recent refurbishment, the Clock Tower is open to the public at selected times, and from its top, offers superb view of North London.

* * *

The Clock Giants of Fleet Street

Standing on an arm protruding from the wall high up on the side of St Dunstan-in-the-West Church in Fleet Street there is a fairly ordinary looking clock, which has a several interesting historical aspects.

It is circular with a diameter of 8 feet, has a black face and gold Roman numerals, and was originally installed into the previous medieval church that stood on this site in 1671, only five years after the Great Fire of London. At that time, it was London's first public clock to have a second hand. When the church was

Giants Gog and Magog stand behind the clock in Fleet Street, ready to strike their bells with clubs every quarter of an hour.

demolished in 1828, the clock was removed and kept by art collector Francis Seymour-Conway in his Regent's Park mansion. More than a century later, it was returned to its rightful place on the side of the rebuilt church in 1935 to mark the Silver Jubilee of King George V.

What marks the clock as being out of the ordinary is the way the hours and quarter hours are struck by two automatons hitting bells with their clubs, in a roofed alcove behind and above the clock. The figures represent Gog and Magog, two giants whose origins are biblical, but who in this context, legend has it, were made guardians of the City of London in Roman times.

Every quarter of an hour, the two automaton giants in the alcove strike the bells with their clubs and turn their heads to gaze east and west along Fleet Street. The clock has featured in many literary works, including *Tom Brown's Schooldays* by Thomas Hughes, *The Vicar of Wakefield* by Oliver Goldsmith and *David Copperfield* by Charles Dickens.

Chapter 8

In Search of Old London Bridge

There has been a bridge across the river Thames at, or close to, the present location right back to the first century, when the Romans built a crossing in or around AD 50. Like the many bridges that followed it, this first one was made of wood, rickety and prone to damage and even destruction, mainly by fire, but also when ships collided with it. This situation continued until medieval times when, in 1176, King Henry II commissioned the building of a far more permanent stone bridge. It took thirty-three years to complete and lasted for more than 600 years.

The structure was supported on nineteen gothic arches, and was nearly 1,000 feet long. Shops and houses up to seven storeys high lined each side, and toilets from some of the buildings overhung the bridge to discharge their waste directly into the river below. In the centre of the bridge there was a chapel, dedicated to St Thomas Becket, the Archbishop of Canterbury until his murder in 1170. The bridge chapel was for the use of pilgrims beginning their pilgrimages from London to Canterbury Cathedral in Kent to visit Becket's tomb. Over the bridge's central arch, higher than the nine on each side, a drawbridge could be raised to allow through the passage of tall-masted ships. Waterwheels and a mill were also to be found on the structure.

Old London Bridge, as depicted by Claude de Jongh in a 1632 oil painting.

In its early days, the design wasn't very practical. The buildings on each side reduced the central roadway to about 13 feet, allowing only enough room for two carriageways that had to carry pedestrians, horses and carts in both directions.

Although a lot more permanent than the old wooden bridges that preceded it, the medieval bridge was not without its problems, and parts of it collapsed on several occasions during its lifetime. The old rhyme *London Bridge is Falling Down* wasn't based specifically on this or any other London bridge, having been adapted originally from an old Norse Saga. But the reference in the rhyme to *My Fair Lady* was added during these years, attributed to Queen Eleanor, who was blamed for misusing revenue gained from the bridge, rather than applying it to its maintenance and repair.

Nevertheless, the bridge lasted until 1799, when building began on a new bridge a little way upstream. That one was opened in 1831 and lasted until 1967, when work began on the current bridge, which was opened in 1973. Its predecessor was sold in 1968 to an American entrepreneur who had it dismantled and shipped brick by brick to Arizona, where it was rebuilt.

It is, however, the medieval bridge that lasted 600 years or more that won the name of Old London Bridge, and it's the remains of this bridge that can still be found scattered around the immediate area where the bridge once crossed the river, as well as a few further flung areas of London.

* * *

The Entrance to the Bridge
On a wall of the church of St Magnus the Martyr in Lower Thames Street there is a plaque that states: 'This churchyard formed part of the roadway approach to Old London Bridge 1176–1831.' Close by, a stone arch built into the base of the church tower and leading into the churchyard was once the pedestrian entrance to Old London Bridge.

A plaque indicates the original use for the tower entrance.

What was once the pedestrian entrance to Old London Bridge.

The church, now a Grade I listed building, was designed in the baroque style by architect Sir Christopher Wren. Since early times, churches supported the building of bridges, which was seen an act of piety. The giving of alms was encouraged so much so that, when Old London Bridge was being built, Londoners gave gifts of land and money to God and the bridge. The bridge was designed and its work supervised by Peter de Colechurch, a priest and head of the Fraternity of the Brethren of London Bridge.

The northern end of the bridge formed a gateway to the City, with the bridge aligned with Fish Street Hill, still to be found behind The Monument. This took pedestrians and horse traffic past the west side of the church. But, following a falling out between the church and the chapel on the bridge itself, the chapel was closed; the church grew more important and was enlarged, so that the archway within its tower became the pedestrian entrance to the bridge.

Horse traffic would have passed onto the bridge from a point to the west of the tower, making this small area and the route across the bridge one of the busiest roads in London. It was said that it could take up to an hour to make the crossing.

Walking through the church tower archway today and into what is now the churchyard beyond gives some idea of just how narrow the roadway across the bridge must have been for the thousands of Londoners who made the crossing.

* * *

The Last of the Arches

In a corner of the churchyard of St Magnus the Martyr, there is a large set of stones, seemingly piled or merely dumped at the spot for no apparent reason. There is no label or other identification that would lead you to believe that they are anything more than miscellaneous lumps of stone or concrete.

In the churchyard, all that remains of one of the bridge's arches.

They are, however, remains of the northernmost arch of the bridge, one of nineteen that would have supported the road at the point where pedestrians emerged from the church's arch and onto the bridge.

* * *

Surviving Shelters

Although the Old London Bridge was completed in 1209, bits and pieces were added over the years, including major reconstruction in the 1700s, when fourteen stone alcoves with pillars on each side, a domed roof on top and a seat running around the interior were installed. Amazingly, four of these still survive and are in daily use as shelters.

The shelter with Keats's statue, in the grounds of Guy's Hospital.

One such alcove-cum-shelter stands in the grounds of Guy's Hospital in Southwark, where it was originally purchased for the use of convalescing patients of the hospital. Unlike the other three, however, this one has a permanent occupant. It is a statue of the English romantic poet John Keats, who sits on the left of the shelter's seat. He is there because, as well as being known as a poet, he was also a one-time medical student at Guy's Hospital, where he assisted surgeons during operations.

A second London Bridge shelter stands rather incongruously in the gardens of the Courtland's Estate, a block of flats in East Sheen. It was originally one of a pair used as porters' lodges, but during renovation work in the 1930s, the second one was lost, along with some balustrade from the original bridge that had been used as part of a wall.

The other two alcoves stand in Victoria Park in East London, where they are still used as shelters by visitors to the park.

* * *

The King's Arms

Unsurprisingly, above the door of the King's Arms pub in Newcomen Street, South London, there is a coat of arms. But despite the pub being a Grade II listed building, the coat of arms didn't start its life here.

The coat of arms from the tollgate, now above a pub entrance in South London.

Originally, it graced the entrance to Stonegate, the toll gate at the southern entrance to Old London Bridge. It was installed during rebuilding in 1728, when King George II was on the throne. When the toll gate was demolished, the coat of arms was shifted to its present position above the door of the appropriately named pub.

* * *

Remains of the New Bridge

The Old London Bridge is not the only one to have left behind a plethora of relics. Remains can also be found of the so-called New London Bridge, which replaced the Old London Bridge in 1831 (and which is in itself old today compared to the current bridge). On the south side of the bridge, across the road from the entrance to London Bridge station, there are two granite stone benches set into the pavement.

But they didn't start their lives as convenient places for weary travellers to sit. These are coping stones from the New Bridge – originally the highest point in a stone building, wall or other structure and used to celebrate the finishing touches being put in place. They were discovered when foundations were being dug for the Southwark Needle sculpture, which now stands at the southern end of the current London Bridge.

The sculpture commemorates the spot where, for 400 years, the heads of traitors,

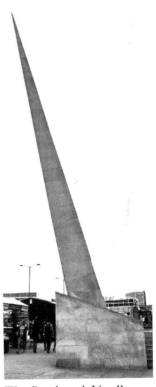

The Southwark Needle commemorates the spot where traitors' heads were displayed on spikes at the southern end of Old London Bridge.

who included William 'Braveheart' Wallace, Guy Fawkes, Wat Tyler and Thomas Cromwell, were gruesomely displayed on spikes during the lifetime of Old London Bridge.

Chapter 9

Tunnels under London

London is riddled with tunnels. Some are no longer in use, with remains that are difficult to find; others are still used daily; and a good few probably never existed in the first place.

An amazing number of rumours and legends have grown up around tunnels under London. Stories proliferate, concerning secret tunnels that linked pubs close to the river in East London that were used by smugglers; tunnels that link government buildings; tunnels from the Houses of Parliament at Westminster to the MI6 headquarters further along the river; a tunnel from the Old Bailey, which stands on the site of the old Newgate Prison, to the church of St Sepulchre used by the clergy to visit condemned men in their cells; and even a tunnel that links Buckingham Palace to the nearest underground railway station in case the monarch needs to make a quick exit. There's a good chance that some tunnels such as these did once exist, or might even still exist, though finding them and proving it is another matter.

The following tunnels, however, do exist, and many are still in use. Even those that can no longer be easily accessed have left behind interesting remains to explore. The first is one such.

* * *

The Thames Tunnel
Brunel Gardens at Rotherhithe in South London is a small patch of green enclosed by a circular wall next to a strange building with a seemingly disproportionately high chimney stack. The wall and the building are all that remains above ground of one of the most ambitious, daring and downright dangerous engineering projects of

The old boiler house used in the construction of the Thames Tunnel now houses the Brunel Museum.

the Victorian age: the excavation and building of the first tunnel in the world to be dug under a navigable river.

The Thames Tunnel stretched from Rotherhithe on the south bank of the river Thames to Wapping, on the north side. It was the brainchild of Marc Brunel, father of engineer Isambard Kingdom Brunel, who joined his father at the age of twenty a year after digging began. Work started in 1825 and didn't finish until 1843.

Brunel first built a huge shaft, 50 feet in diameter, 150 feet back from the south bank of the river. The shaft was built like a tower above ground in the form of a circular 3-foot wide brick wall, 42 feet high, on top of a sharpened steel rim. It weighed about 1,000 tons, and once

Anne Perry

built, the whole thing was allowed to sink into the ground under its own weight. Inside, men at the base worked to excavate the earth that built up as the tower sunk, whilst a steam engine at the top pumped out water that filled the bottom. Once it had sunk to the required depth, miners at the base began digging through the thick sludge, out and under the river.

With setbacks that included major leaks and floods that claimed lives, financial problems and a period when work was forced to stop for seven years, it took eighteen years to complete, when it was proclaimed the Eighth Wonder of the World.

The remains of the shaft's walls now form the circular enclosure around the gardens, while the strange building nearby was originally the boiler house that drove the steam pumps used in the excavation. The building now houses the Brunel Museum, dedicated to telling the story of how the tunnel was built.

The Thames Tunnel was originally envisaged for use by horse-drawn vehicles, but lack of finances prevented the building of spiral ramps in the shafts that would have been needed for the purpose. It was, however, used by pedestrians until 1865, when it was sold to

The circular wall and fence that today encloses a small garden was once the top of that shaft that led to the tunnel.

How the tunnel looked below ground when it was opened in 1843.

a railway company. The tunnel remains today, used by the London Overground railway. Although there is no longer public access to the tunnel itself, it is possible to access the shaft from within the Brunel Museum – and to sit on top of it in the gardens that its rim encloses.

* * *

Greenwich Foot Tunnel

Right back to Roman times, when London was called Londinium, and on through the years, the river Thames has always presented an inconvenient barrier dividing the City in two. Bridges, ferries and tunnels have all been used to link the two river banks. The Greenwich Foot Tunnel was opened in 1902 for pedestrians, and it is still in use today.

The tunnel links Greenwich, close to the *Cutty Sark*, the recently restored British clipper ship on permanent display here, with Island Gardens at the southern end of the Isle of Dogs. The entrances at each end of the tunnel are in the form of circular brick buildings topped with impressive glazed domes. Inside each one, lifts and circular staircases give pedestrians access to the circular tunnel, which runs

The Greenwich foot tunnel, which runs under the river.

at about 50 feet below the river. The tunnel is more than 1,200 feet long, made from cast iron lined with concrete with a diameter of approximately 9 feet, and its walls are lined with about 200,000 tiles.

The southern entrance to the tunnel at Greenwich.

Greenwich Foot Tunnel was designed by Sir Alexander Binnie, the Chief Engineer for London County Council, whose other design accomplishments included Blackwall Tunnel, built in 1897 for vehicular traffic in East London, and Vauxhall Bridge, which was opened in 1906. The tunnel replaced a ferry service, which was reputed to be not only unreliable, but also expensive. Its principal use when it was opened was to help workers in South London get to their places of work in the London Docks and shipyards north of the river.

Today, the Greenwich Foot Tunnel is classed as a public highway and is therefore open to the public twenty-four hours a day.

* * *

Woolwich Foot Tunnel

Woolwich is most famous for its ferry, which dates way back to 1308, but which was most notable for its fleet of boats that resembled Mississippi paddle steamers that began plying their trade in 1889.

The Woolwich foot tunnel.

Those boats would be London curiosities in themselves today had more modern diesel vessels not replaced them in 1963. The early ferries were much used to give local workers access to the docks and shipyards on the north bank of the Thames, but were unreliable due to fog that frequently shrouded the area in the nineteenth century.

In their place a foot tunnel was begun in 1876, but never completed. The one that was completed and is still open today was begun in 1910 and finished a year later. It was designed by Irish engineer Maurice Fitzmaurice, who took over from the Greenwich

The wood-panelled lift that carries passengers down to the tunnel at Woolwich.

Foot Tunnel designer Alexander Binnie when he retired from his position with London County Council.

The Woolwich Tunnel was dug by hand and made up of a series of cast-iron rings joined together. Working in shifts, the tunnellers dug at the rate of about 8 feet every twenty-four hours.

The entrances on each bank are red brick rotundas with conical roofs. Canopied doorways lead to spiral staircases and huge, wood-panelled electric lifts capable of carrying forty passengers at a time. The tunnel runs under the river at a depth of nearly 65 feet.

At more than 1,600 feet in length, it is longer than its neighbouring tunnel in Greenwich and open to both pedestrians and cyclists.

* * *

The Camden Catacombs

Deep beneath the streets of Camden Town, under its famous market and winding around under a lot more of the area, there is a network of underground passages and vaults, a vast subterranean hall and even a canal basin. Although the term is not strictly accurate, since no dead bodies are stored here, they have become known as the Camden catacombs.

The tunnels were excavated in the nineteenth century, primarily as storage areas and stables for pit ponies and horses working on the nearby canal, and also to shunt railway wagons. The large hall beneath the ground once housed a steam-powered winding mechanism that was used to haul trains up the steep hill from Euston station.

The canal basin is still visible from the canal close to Camden Lock, and a brief glimpse of the catacombs can be seen from Camden's Stables Market.

The catacombs are no longer open to the public. It is possible, however, to trace their routes beneath the streets of Camden by following a line of cast-iron grills set into the road surfaces. Originally,

Part of the catacombs that run under Camden.

these were the only source of light to the tunnels, which, in the days when they were in use, brought together the three big Victorian means of transport: horses, waterways and railways.

* * *

The Tower Subway

At Tower Hill, close to the Tower of London, there is a circular brick building that houses the entrance to a tunnel built between 1869 and 1870. Its purpose was to convey passengers under the river Thames while sitting in a wooden tram-like carriage that was hauled on cables from one end to the other.

Passengers descended a spiral staircase, or used a lift that held six people at a time, taking them to a waiting room below ground and thence into the tunnel, which was circular, made of iron, 7 feet in diameter and about a quarter of a

The entrance to the Tower Subway, built in the 1920s.

mile in length. The carriage in which they sat ran on narrow-gauge tracks. It seated fourteen people and was controlled by a driver who had access to brakes, but no means of motion. It was propelled entirely by means of the engine that pulled the cables that towed it through the tunnel, and gravity from the incline of the tunnel itself from each end to its centre.

There were two classes. First class passengers paid tuppence (two pennies in pre-decimal currency) and second class passengers paid one penny. First class passengers were given priority in use of the lifts, which carried fewer than half the number of people that could be carried in the carriage.

The service ran for less than a year, when it became uneconomical to carry on running the carriages. The tracks were scrapped and the tunnel opened to pedestrians, who were charged a ha'penny (half a penny) for the privilege of making the journey by foot. It could not have been a very comfortable walk, since the tunnel's dimensions caused tall people to stoop and the gas lighting along its length kept the ambient temperature high. People who suffered from chest complaints were advised not to make the journey

The original tunnel entrance was square with an overhanging pitched roof. The tunnel closed in 1898, after which it was used for hydraulic mains power tubes and water mains. The circular brick building that stands on Tower Hill today was built in the 1920s by the London Hydraulic Power Company, whose name is seen around its circumference. The tunnel is still used to carry telecommunications cables.

* * *

Clapham Station Bunker

Between 1941 and 1942, during the Second World War, eight deep level shelters were dug under London underground stations for the purposes of sheltering Londoners from air raids. The one at Clapham station is now open to the public to see what life was like underground during the days of the blitz.

The bunker is accessed through a circular rotunda building on Clapham Common, from where steps take visitors down to below the level of the underground railway at this spot. The bunker actually comprises two tunnels, each one 17 feet in diameter and 1,600 feet in length. It originally housed 8,000 bunks.

What was once the safe haven of thousands of Londoners during German bombing raids has now become something of a tourist attraction, complete with a café in the rotunda entrance.

* * *

The Albert Memorial Undercroft

The Albert Memorial, one of the best known monuments in London, has a secret underground existence in the form of an undercroft of brick arched tunnels forming vaults, similar to the crypt of a church. The tunnels are accessed by a manhole in front of the memorial.

The crypt-like undercroft beneath the Albert Memorial.

The undercroft stands on top of the memorial's 17-foot foundations. It comprises more than 850 brick arches, at the centre of which a brick column supports the bronze statue of Albert, in the middle of the memorial above ground. The marble steps that ascend to the memorial outside are actually laid on top of the undercroft's arches. The height from floor to roof is less at the northern end than at the southern end, due to the way the ground slopes.

The marble steps that lead up to the Albert Memorial are laid directly onto the roofs of the undercroft arches.

The few people who have been privileged to visit the Albert Memorial undercroft have reported it to be claustrophobic, and just a little spooky, even though it does have its own lighting and even heating to prevent water drainage pipes from freezing in the winter.

Unfortunately, the undercroft is no longer open to the public, except by special and rare guided tours.

* * *

Buried Streets

If you stand on a traffic island in the middle of Charring Cross Road close to Cambridge Circus, and look into the iron grill set into the paving stones, you might see what appears to be another buried street, complete with two street signs on a wall.

The signs tell you this was Little Compton Street, which once connected Old Compton Street at its junction with Charring Cross Road, to New Compton Street. It is sometimes stated that this is the actual street, which was buried when Charring Cross Road was created in the 1890s.

In fact, it isn't the street itself, but the utility tunnel, once part of a greater complex that ran under the old, now forgotten road.

The difference between the truth of the utility tunnel and the romance of a real buried street is typical of the many urban myths that

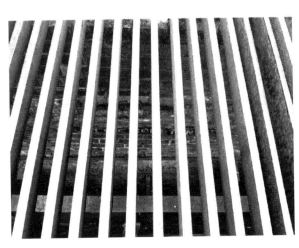

What remains of Little Compton Street, buried under Charing Cross Road.

have grown up around the idea of buried streets under London. One of the most popular is that there is a tunnel beneath the Selfridges department store in Oxford Street that reveals the original street that was buried when the present one was built. Those who believe in such matters will tell you that here you will find a complete underground Victorian street, with period shop frontages still intact on each side.

It's one of those stories that is usually narrated by someone who knows someone else, who knows someone who once saw it. Its actual existence is yet to be verified.

* * *

Lost Rivers

Outside St Pancras Old Church in Pancras Road, a plaque shows people bathing on the banks of a river at this spot. It seems somewhat incongruous in such a traffic-congested place where there is no sign of any water. But the plaque refers to the way things were in the early nineteenth century, when there was a river here. It was the river

The plaque outside St Pancras Old Church, which shows bathers in the river Fleet.

Fleet, and it's still there, buried underground – just like so many of London's lost rivers.

Time was when London was criss-crossed by a great many rivers, most of which led to the Thames. But in medieval times and then on into the Victorian era, as the City was developed, the majority of these were covered, diverted, buried or incorporated into London's sewer system. Today, little evidence remains of rivers like the Fleet, Effram, Neckinger, Tyburn, Walbrook and Westbourne, although if you know where to look, traces can still be found of some before they disappear underground.

Both ends of the river Fleet can be seen, first at the spot where it rises at Hampstead and Highgate Ponds, to flow underground before being dispersed into the Thames at Blackfriars.

The Effra was a South London river that today travels underground beneath Dulwich, Herne Hill and Brixton before meeting the Thames near Vauxhall Bridge.

The mouth of the river Fleet, where it enters the Thames under Blackfriars Bridge.

A little way east of Tower Bridge, the river Neckinger empties into the Thames after journeying from its source in Southwark. The Tyburn, which once ran from Regent's Park, through Marylebone and along Oxford Street, was diverted in medieval times through a pipe that took it to Cheapside, where it was used as a source of drinking water.

The Walbrook runs under Walbrook Street on its way to the Thames. The Westbourne, which starts in Hampstead and once fed the Serpentine in Hyde Park before being converted into a sewer, meets the Thames at Chelsea.

Other lost, forgotten or buried rivers of London include the river Moselle, Muswell Stream, Counter's Creek, Stamford Brook, river Brent, river Rom, Earl's Sluice, river Peck, the Falconbrook, river Graveney, river Quaggy, Beverley Brook and Sudbrook.

Some of these latter rivers, in part at least, are still evident above ground. It is, however, all but impossible today, short of descending below ground, often into the London sewers, to see evidence of most of the others. Even so, the names of many of London's lost, buried and forgotten rivers live on in the names of roads that follow their nearby original courses: Moselle Street, Muswell Road, Effra Road, Walbrook Street, Westbourne Grove, Neckinger, Fleet Street, Fleet Road and Old Fleet Lane.

* * *

London's Other Underground Railway

The London Underground, which operates close to 250 miles of track to carry about 1.1 billion passengers a year, is world famous. Lesser known is London's other underground railway that once ran under the streets of the capital to support a fleet of miniature driverless trains. The trains no longer run, but the tunnels are still there.

This is the London Post Office Railway, otherwise known as Mail Rail. Its origins lie in Victorian times, when the build-up of horse-drawn vehicles cluttered London roads to such an extent that the Post

One of the miniature driverless trains once operated by the Post Office.

Office set out to find new and faster ways to transport letters and parcels to its eight sorting offices. The answer was to build its own underground railway network specifically for the purpose.

As far back as 1839, consideration was given to a pneumatic railway that used huge fans to blow carriages through pipes under the ground. But it wasn't until 1913 that work began on a more practical method using electric trains. By 1917, the tunnels had been completed, but resources were low due to the ongoing First World War, and the scheme came to a halt. Until the end of hostilities the tunnels were used by the National Portrait Gallery, among others, to store and protect national treasures and works of art.

The system finally opened to carry mail in 1927. It was the world's first electric railway with driverless trains. At its peak the system ran for twenty-two hours a day, carrying as many as four million letters every day. It ran from Paddington to Whitechapel, serving stations in between at Bird Street, Wimpole Street, Rathbone Place, New Oxford Street, Mount Pleasant, King Edward Street and Liverpool Street.

Mail Rail ran until 2003, when new technologies made it redundant. When it was closed, the tunnels were sealed off, although a small group of engineers was maintained to service the system.

Now, for the first time, part of the network has been opened to the public, who are able to ride in carriages converted from the old rolling stock. Access is via the Postal Museum in Phoenix Place, from where passengers are invited to ride on a short loop of track deep below Mount Pleasant, once one of the largest sorting offices in the world.

* * *

Chislehurst's Man-Made Caves

About 100 feet beneath Chislehurst, in the South East London Borough of Bromley, there exists a labyrinth of tunnels that stretches for 22 miles. Although known as the Chislehurst Caves, they are actually man-made passages, dating back to the middle of the thirteenth century.

The caves were originally dug for mining chalk, used in lime burning and brick laying for the building of London. Flint was also mined here, for use in tinderboxes and flintlock guns.

Chislehurst Caves, buried deep beneath the streets of a London suburb.

The caves are split into three sections named Saxon, Druid and Roman, named after the people who, legend has it, played a part in digging them. Each section is joined by further passages, which were added after the original excavations.

The caves were probably last used for mining purposes in the mid-nineteenth century. Since then, they have served a number of different purposes, including use as an ammunition depot during the First World War, and later, for the cultivation of mushrooms. During the Second World War they became almost an underground town as one of the largest deep air raid shelters in the UK. At the height of the bombing, more than 15,000 people sheltered here. In more recent times the caves have been put to use as music venues and as unusual and weird locations for films and television programmes.

Today, Chislehurst Caves are a major tourist attraction in this part of London. Lamplit guided tours are offered every hour, but visitors are advised to stay close to the guides to prevent getting lost in the tunnels. Those who suffer from claustrophobia or fear of the dark are advised not to take the tour.

Chapter 10

Peculiar Parks

London has eight Royal parks: Hyde Park, Kensington Gardens, Green Park, Regent's Park and St James's Park in Central London, with Bushy Park, Greenwich Park and Richmond Park in the suburbs. The capital also has numerous lesser-known parks – and it's in these that you find the most curiosities.

* * *

Crystal Palace Park

There is a park in South London that contains huge models of prehistoric creatures, numerous headless statues and grand staircases leading nowhere. They are all that remains of the Crystal Palace, the world's largest glass building, erected originally to house The Great Exhibition of 1851.

The rebuilt Crystal Palace that stood in South London in 1854.

When the exhibition ended, the Palace was taken apart and transported piece by piece to the top of Sydenham Hill in South London, where it was rebuilt at the centre of a kind of Victorian theme park. It burned down in 1936, leaving behind a park full of curiosities.

Meet the creator

One of the park's curiosities is a huge five-times life-size stone effigy of Sir Joseph Paxton unveiled in 1873 to commemorate his role as architect of the original Crystal Palace, as well as being responsible for its reincarnation in South London.

Paxton was Head Gardner at Chatsworth House, the Duke of Devonshire's country house in Derbyshire, where, among other things, he designed a large glass house that became known as The Great Conservatory. It was this that influenced the design of the Crystal Palace.

Based on doodles he made on a piece of blotting paper during a business meeting, Paxton engaged a small team and together they worked day and night to complete the plans for the original building in just nine days.

A gigantic bust of Sir Joseph Paxton stands today with his back to the remains of the Crystal Palace.

The monsters by the lake

Along the banks of the park's lake, in the water and emerging from the shrubbery are huge models of prehistoric creatures with names like plesiosaurus and ichthyosaurus. Walking along the pathways around the lake takes you through a timeline of the different types of creature seen through three prehistoric eras.

Originally unveiled in 1854, they were the work of sculptor and natural history artist Benjamin Waterhouse Hawkins. Six years before the publication of Charles Darwin's *On the Origin of Species*, the huge models were based on scientific knowledge of the time and created a sensation among Victorian visitors to the park.

Prehistoric monsters roam the waters and shrubbery around the lake.

They were classed as Grade II listed in 1973, restored in 2002 and upgraded to Grade I listed in 2007.

Statues, staircases and forgotten fountains

When it was rebuilt in South London, the Crystal Palace was surrounded by a landscape of terraces, statues, ornamental English and Italian style gardens, and the country's largest maze. At each

An impressive staircase leads up to terraces that are part of what little remains of the great building today.

A headless statue stands guard over stone arches alongside the steps.

side of the building huge water towers provided the volume and pressure of water required to power fountains that were said to rival those at the French Palace of Versailles.

The maze is still there but empty plinths are all that remain of a great many of the marble statues, and those that have survived are mostly headless. They lead the way to an impressive staircase, with stone arches on each side. One wide flight of steps is flanked on each side by a stone sphinx, just two of twelve that once stood at the entrances to the Crystal Palace.

The entrance to the maze that still remains.

* * *

Victoria Park

Victoria Park was the first in the world to be built solely for the needs of surrounding communities. Now situated in the London Borough of Tower Hamlets, this is today London's oldest public park. The building of the park was decreed by an Act of Parliament in 1841, when London's East End was a slum area, full of unhealthy industry and a population of 400,000. For many of the people who lived in London's East End at this time, it was the only stretch of uninterrupted greenery they had ever seen. Today, the park contains three unusual structures.

A giant of a drinking fountain

Standing beside the lake is one of the most ornate drinking fountains in London. It's huge, made from pink marble, granite and stone, with six Gothic arches and festooned with sculptures of cherubs. Four clocks sit in the cupola, which forms the slate roof that is topped by a weather vane.

The huge and ornate drinking fountain in Victoria Park.

The fountain was erected in 1842 at the behest of wealthy philanthropist Baroness Burdett-Coutts, to supply clean drinking water for both people and animals, supported by the Metropolitan Drinking Fountain and Cattle Trough Association, a body that provided water troughs for cattle and horses.

Designed by architect Henry Astley Darbishire, the fountain cost £6,000 to build. It was restored as part of a general restoration of Victoria Park between January 2011 and July 2012.

A little bit of Old London Bridge

A rare remnant of the old London Bridge, now used as a park shelter.

Visitors who need a rest while strolling through the park might find themselves sitting on a seat within one of two large stone domed arches.

Each of these arches came from the remains of the old London Bridge that was demolished in 1831, when parts were sold off to be utilised elsewhere. They were originally two of fourteen shelters added to the bridge during its reconstruction in the 1700s and have stood in the park since Victorian times.

China comes to London

When China opened its doors to the West in Victorian times, London went wild for all things Chinese. That included a Chinese exhibition in Hyde Park whose

The new Chinese Pagoda that replaced the original damaged in the Second World War.

entrance was dominated by a large pagoda. When the exhibition closed, the pagoda was purchased, dismantled and rebuilt on an island in the middle of the lake in Victoria Park.

Unfortunately, this was an area of London that was heavily bombed during the Second World War, and the original pagoda was badly damaged as a result. The one that stands at the same location today was built as part of the major renovation work in 2011–12 that also renovated the water fountain.

* * *

King Edward VII Memorial Park

King George V and Queen Mary opened this park in 1922, dedicating it to the memory of King Edward VII, who died in 1910. In many ways, it's a typical East London park – apart from a couple of curiosities.

It's not a church, it's a ventilation shaft

Beside a path that runs alongside the river Thames that borders the park, there is a building that looks like a circular brick-built church with twin entry doors and ornate iron grills on the windows. Closer examination reveals that the ironwork on the windows spells out

Looking more like a church than a ventilation shaft, the peculiar brick-built structure in King Edward VII Memorial Park.

the letters 'LCC', standing for London County Council, which was formed in 1889

The building and its twin on the opposite bank of the river are sometimes referred to as the Rotherhithe Rotunda. They are, in fact, ventilation shafts for the Rotherhithe Tunnel, which runs below the park. Inside, large fans extract noxious fumes from the tunnel below, these days from car exhausts, but originally for the more organic consequences of so much underground horse-drawn activity.

The entry doors, which lead to disused staircases down to the tunnel, were used when it was opened in 1908 by workmen whose job was to descend into the tunnel and spend their day walking its length shovelling up the growing mountains of horse manure that soiled the underground road. There must have been worse jobs in London at the time, but it's difficult to envisage what they could have been.

An unusual memorial

On the north side of the ventilation shaft stands a ceramic and stone memorial that was erected by London County Council in 1922. It reads:

> This tablet is in memory of Sir Hugh Willoughby, Stephen Borough, William Borough, Sir Martin Frobisher and other navigators who, in the latter half of the sixteenth century, set sail from this reach of the river Thames near Ratcliff Cross to explore the Northern Seas.

The memorial to the sixteenth-century navigators, erected beside the shaft.

Sir Hugh Willoughby was the captain of a ship called the *Bona Esperanza*, who set out, along with other ships under his command, in 1553. Separated by terrible storms, Willoughby managed to get his ship into a bay at what is today Finland. He and his crew were found by Russian fishermen a year later frozen to death.

* * *

Brunel Gardens Park

Close to the banks of the river Thames at Rotherhithe stands a miniature park, no more than a small and rather overgrown garden contained within a perfectly circular wall. Nearby stands an odd building, strange machinery and curious seating. The clue to there being so many oddities in such a small space lies in the name associated with the gardens: Brunel.

The building houses the Brunel Museum, dedicated to the work of Isambard Kingdom Brunel, one of the Victorian age's greatest engineers, and his father Marc, who were both heavily involved in building the Thames Tunnel.

The small, circular garden that stands at the top of the shaft that originally led down to the tunnel excavation.

The wall around the circular gardens marks the outer perimeter of the shaft that was sunk here in 1825 at the start of the tunnel's excavation. But in the area that surrounds the museum building there are other curiosities associated with the Brunel name.

Benches and seats were designed and made to resemble bridges built by Isambard Brunel. They include the Maidenhead Bridge on the Great Western Railway, which was completed in 1838; Hungerford Suspension Bridge, Brunel's first bridge across the Thames, completed in 1846; and the Royal Albert Bridge, Brunel's last bridge, which spans the river Tamar, dividing Devon and Cornwall, and opened in 1859.

Seats made to look like Royal Albert Bridge (top) and Hungerford Suspension Bridge (below).

Isambard Brunel's last project was the design of the SS *Great Eastern*, an iron steam ship that was the largest ever built at the time of its launch in 1858. The ship was built at Millwall, only a few miles from Rotherhithe, and the huge piece of machinery that stands in the Museum Gardens is an original grinding wheel used in the construction of the giant ship.

* * *

Part of a grinding wheel used in the construction of the SS *Great Eastern*.

China Comes to Kew

The Royal Botanic Gardens at Kew – more usually known simply as Kew Gardens – was founded in 1759 and today contains the world's largest collection of living plants. It is also famous for its iconic glass plant houses. Less well known is the little bit of China that made its way to Kew in 1762.

The Chinese pagoda in Kew Gardens.

The Chinese pagoda that stands in the south-east corner of the botanical gardens was designed by London-based Scottish-Swedish architect Sir William Chambers. The pagoda and other exotic buildings erected at the time were in homage to the Grand Tour – a traditional trip around the sites of Europe regularly taken by the rich upper classes.

This was a time when Britain had a big thing for all things Chinese and the pagoda at Kew was one of the wonders of London. At 164 feet high and octagonal in shape, it incorporated ten floors with protruding roofs, and with each successive floor being 1 foot less in height and diameter than the one below. Originally it was very colourful, covered in varnished iron plates and decorated with eight wooden dragons gilded with gold.

Over the years the dragons rotted and disappeared, but have now been replaced as part of a major renovation project, which at last sees the pagoda returned to its eighteenth-century splendour.

* * *

The Park of Unsung Heroes

Close to St Paul's Cathedral, two churchyards and a graveyard form the basis of a small park, well known as a haven of quiet in the midst of the busy City. It is called Postman's Park, a name derived from its popularity as a lunchtime venue among workers from the General Post Office Headquarters that stood in St Martin's Le Grand until its closure in 1910.

The area, which is bordered by Aldersgate Street, St. Martin's Le Grand, King Edward Street and Little Britain, was laid out as a public garden in 1880. It peculiarity is a rather touching memorial that was unveiled there in 1900 at the instigation George Frederick Watts.

Watts was a popular painter and sculptor of the Victorian era. In 1887 he wrote a letter to *The Times* newspaper suggesting a novel way to celebrate Queen Victoria's golden jubilee. His idea was to build a memorial to unsung heroes, or, as he put it in his letter, 'heroism in everyday life'.

The result is the memorial that still stands in the park today. It consists of a wooden shelter that protects fifty-four memorial tablets commemorating sixty-two men, women and children who gave their lives in the course of trying to protect others.

Some of the memorial tablets to be found at Postman's Park.

Watts was inspired to create the memorial as a record of ordinary people, none of them famous, who might otherwise be forgotten. He also wanted it to be instructional and to offer examples of what he believed to be appropriate and moral behaviour for those who wished to live as respectable and honourable citizens.

To choose the people to be commemorated, Watts collected newspaper reports of heroic acts, from which suitable cases were chosen. His wife Mary, working with a committee from the nearby St Botolph's Church, continued collecting information after Watts's death in 1904.

Among the tablets on display today, you'll find epitaphs to 17-year-old Elizabeth Boxall, who died in 1888 'of injuries received in trying to save a child from a runaway horse'; pantomime artist Sarah Smith, who died in 1863 'when attempting in her inflammable dress to extinguish the flames which had enveloped her companion'; and 61-year-old Daniel Pemberton, who, in 1903, was 'surprised by a train when gauging the line, hurled his mate out of the track, saving his life at the cost of his own'.

The tablets were installed mostly in the early 1900s, but one as late as 2009. The tablets in the middle row, the first of the three to be installed, were manufactured by William De Morgan, an English potter, tile designer and novelist. The top and bottom rows were made predominantly by Doulton of Lambeth.

Chapter 11

Monuments and Memorials

There are countless monuments and memorials in London, but not all are what they seem. They range from miniature models of famous buildings to tributes to people and events that you might never have heard of. Even those memorials that you thought you knew everything about have secrets to reveal. Here are some of the more unusual, obscure and surprising monuments and memorials that you'll find scattered around the capital.

* * *

Alfred Hitchcock in London

Alfred Hitchcock, one of America's most famous film directors, was born in London, where he worked for the early part of his career. He was born in 1899 in Leytonstone, at 517 High Street. Nearby are several memorials to the man who later emigrated to America to become known as the Master of Suspense.

Hitchcock in East London

The flat over a greengrocer's shop where Hitchcock was born no longer exists. It is now the site of a petrol station, but fixed to the rear wall of the forecourt there is a blue plaque erected by Waltham Forest Heritage. It states: 'Alfred Joseph Hitchcock.

A plaque in a petrol station celebrates the birthplace of film director Alfred Hitchcock.

The famous film director was born near this site at 517 High Road, Leytonstone on August 13th 1899, died April 24th 1980.'

To the right of the petrol station, there is a white building comprising flats and shops on which has been painted a large mural of flying birds. They were created by painter Mateusz Odrobny, who worked with illustrator Anna Mill. Along with more birds inset into the paving stones in front of the building, they are there to pay homage to one of Hitchcock's most famous films, *The Birds*, made in 1963.

One of Hitchcock's most famous trademarks was to make a fleeting personal appearance in each of his films, and the mural honours that with a portrait of the director inset into the eye of the largest bird in the mural. From a distance, it looks like a light reflection, and can only be properly seen in close up.

Remembering one of Hitchcock's most famous films, a mural of birds decorates a building in Leytonstone.

In front of the bird building, more birds are embedded in the paving stones.

Nearby Leytonstone Underground station also pays tribute to the film director with seventeen mosaics set into the walls of its entrance. Each one depicts a scene from one of Hitchcock's most famous films, including some of his cameo appearances. The films illustrated are *Rebecca*, *The Wrong Man*, *Rear Window*, *North by Northwest*, *The*

Mosaics at Leytonstone Underground Station.

Marnie Court in Leytonstone, named after a Hitchcock film.

Skin Game, Suspicion, Psycho, Number 17, To Catch a Thief, The Birds, Saboteur, Vertigo, Strangers on a Train and *Pleasure Garden*. Three other mosaics show Hitchcock in action directing a film, Hitchcock with Marlene Dietrich, and the young Hitchcock outside his father's greengrocer's shop.

The mosaics were instigated in 1999 to mark the 100th anniversary of the director's birth and were finally unveiled in 2001. They were made by the Greenwich Mural Workshop, took seven months to complete and used more than 80,000 tiles.

Other Hitchcock references in and around the same area include a block of flats called Marnie Court, named after the film *Marnie*; paintings of scenes from Hitchcock films in a wooden showcase; a road called Gainsborough Road, named after the film studios where Hitchcock began his career; and, occasionally, posters announcing seasons of Hitchcock

A painting depicting James Stewart in the Hitchcock film *Rear Window*, displayed near the underground station.

Gainsborough Road, named after the film studios where Hitchcock began his career.

Posters advertising a season of Hitchcock films to be shown at St John's Church in Leytonstone.

films, often in incongruous settings such as St John's Church, near the underground station.

Hitchcock in North London

Alfred Hitchcock began his movie career in England at Gainsborough Studios, where today there is a huge memorial to him.

Gainsborough Studios were in business from 1924 to 1951 and best known for melodramas produced in the 1940s. It was here that Hitchcock made his first suspense thriller, *The Lodger*, in 1926.

Production came to a halt in 1949, and the studios remained empty until the area started to become more fashionable when, in 2001, the old studios were demolished to make way for blocks of luxury flats. But the memory of Hitchcock lives on.

In the central courtyard of the flats, on a sloped plinth surrounded by small trees there is now a huge sculpture of Hitchcock's head. The sculptor was Anthony Donaldson, famous for his simplification of female figures.

A huge bust of Alfred Hitchcock's head gazes out close to the site of the old Gainsborough film studios.

The Hitchcock sculpture is heavy-lidded and almost Buddha-like with an enigmatic smile. Some say its expression illustrates the somewhat casual attitude the director took towards his actors, particularly in directing Margaret Lockwood in *The Lady Vanishes*, his last film at Gainsborough. The sculpture faces west, towards America, where Hitchcock would become most famous.

Nearby, in Shoreditch Park there is a sculpture by abstract painter and sculptor John Edwards, who died in 2009. It's in the form of a huge film reel that formerly stood on the corner of Leonard Street and Paul Street, about a mile away. Moved to its present, more appropriate, position close to the site of the old film studios, the sculpture is called *Hitchcock's Reel*.

Hitchcock's Reel in Shoreditch Park.

Hitchcock in West London

From 1926 to 1939, during the time that Hitchcock worked at Gainsborough Studios, he lived at Cromwell Road in Kensington. Today, his old house has been split into flats. A British Heritage blue plaque on the wall beside a ground floor window states: 'Sir Alfred Hitchcock, 1899–1980, Film Director, lived here 1926–1939.'

A plaque on a house in Kensington celebrates the place where Hitchcock lived during his London film career.

* * *

The Miniature St Paul's

St Paul's Cathedral was built between 1675 and 1710 after its predecessor was destroyed in the Great Fire of London. Until 1962, it was the tallest building in London. St Paul's is one of London's most famous landmarks, but how many know that there is a miniature version of the cathedral on a bridge overlooking the river Thames 3 miles away?

Vauxhall Bridge was opened in 1906. It's Grade II listed, comprises five arches, made of iron and spans the river between Vauxhall and Pimlico. During its design it was proposed to add some ornamentation in the form of statues. The first idea was to erect two 60-foot towers at one end of the bridge with a statue of some kind at the top of each. The idea was rejected as being too expensive.

Consultation with architect Richard Norman Shaw, best known for designing commercial buildings and country houses, came up with the idea of positioning eight bronze statues between the arches, each depicting a different aspect of the British way of life. The sculptors chosen for the task were Londoners Frederick Pomeroy and Alfred Drury.

Pomeroy's statues on the upstream side of the bridge depict pottery, engineering, architecture and agriculture. Drury's statues on the downstream side depict education, fine arts, science and local government.

The miniature model of St Paul's Cathedral is held in one hand of Pomeroy's *Statue of Architecture*. The subject is a young and beautiful woman. In one hand she holds a pair of compasses. The other holds the 2-foot long model of St Paul's.

The other seven statues are equally interesting. The *Statue of Pottery* holds a large, classical pot; the *Statue of Engineering* holds a small steam engine; the *Statue of Agriculture* carries a scythe and a sheaf of corn; the *Statue of Education* is seen as a mother with two children; the *Statue of Fine Arts* holds a painter's palette and brushes; the *Statue of Science* holds an astronomical globe;

A miniature model of St Paul's Cathedral is held by a statue on Vauxhall Bridge.

and the *Statue of Local Government* holds a law book.

The statues are often overlooked by passers-by since they cannot be easily observed from the bridge itself. They can be seen from the north and south banks, but are best viewed from a boat on the river.

* * *

London's Smallest Memorial

Two mice fighting over a piece of cheese can be found on the side of a building on the corner of Philpot Lane at Eastcheap in East London. It is one of, if not the, smallest statues in London, and it dates back to 1862. No one seems to know why they are there, but there are a couple of suppositions.

One theory is that the mice were sculpted for spice merchants Hunt and Crombie, for whom the building, housing the company's offices and warehouse, was built.

A rather more fanciful theory suggests that the tiny statue was erected in memory of two builders who had been working on the construction of the Monument, the memorial to the Great Fire of London, which was erected nearby. The story has it that the two builders got into a fight when one accused the other of stealing his cheese sandwich. During the scuffle both fell to their deaths before mice were identified as the real culprits.

It would be nice to believe the story, but it's difficult to imagine why the architects of a Victorian building erected in the early 1860s would bother to commemorate the lives of two unknown builders working on the Monument, which was opened nearly 200 years earlier in 1677.

* * *

The Centre of London

How is the distance to London from any other place calculated? Some think it takes its measurement from the location of a signpost to the city's nearest boundary, but with a total area of more than 600 square miles, that would clearly be impractical, not to say inaccurate. So to state the number of miles to London, from anywhere in the country, the distance must be calculated by a theoretical journey that ends at one specific spot. That spot is the one that is now accepted as the centre of London.

It's marked by a statue of King Charles I, just south of Trafalgar Square. Set in the ground, close to the rear of the statue, there is a small

The statue of King Charles I at the south of Trafalgar Square stands at the centre of London.

A plaque in the ground close to the statue denotes the place to which distances to London are measured.

brass plaque that's easy to miss unless you look for it. The wording on the plaque states:

> City of Westminster. On the site now occupied by the statue of King Charles was erected the original Queen Eleanor's Cross, a replica of which stands in front of Charing Cross station. Mileages from London are measured from the site of the original cross.

The origins of this marker go back to 1290, when Queen Eleanor, travelling to meet her husband, King Edward in Scotland, fell ill and died near Lincoln. The grieving king decreed that twelve memorial crosses should be erected along the route of the Queen's funeral procession from Lincoln to Westminster Abbey, where she would receive a state burial.

The twelve crosses were erected at Lincoln, Grantham, Stamford, Geddington, Hardingstone, Stony Stratford, Woburn, Dunstable, St Albans, Waltham, Cheapside and Charing Cross, the last two in London. The crosses were made of stone with carvings of the Queen on each of their faces.

The final cross was erected where the statue of King Charles I stands in what is now Trafalgar Square. The square itself didn't come into existence until the 1800s, and is marked by Nelson's Column, erected in 1843 in honour of Admiral Horatio Nelson, who died at the Battle of Trafalgar in 1805.

Only three of Queen Eleanor's crosses remain, at Geddington, Hardingstone and Waltham. The one outside Charing Cross station, a short walk from Trafalgar Square, is a replica, erected in 1863 and probably more ornate than the original.

Modern mapping techniques have identified the exact centre point of London as a spot marked by an anonymous looking bench about half a mile from Trafalgar Square, on the Thames Embankment in front of King's College London, but it is doubtful that signposts throughout the country will ever be changed to reflect that. Traditionally, the centre of London remains to the south of Trafalgar Square.

Queen Eleanor's Cross at Charing Cross is a nineteenth-century replica of the original placed nearby in the thirteenth century.

* * *

The Panyer Boy of Panyer Alley

If you want confirmation of what was once thought to be the highest point in London, look no further than the wall near St Paul's Underground station. There you will find a plaque depicting a young boy sitting on an upturned bread basket, endeavouring to dislodge something, a thorn maybe, from his foot. Beneath the effigy are the words 'When ye have sought the city round, yet this is the highest ground.' The inscription is dated August 1688.

The claim for this to be the highest point in London dates back to Roman times, when Londinium, as it was then known, was built on two hills, namely Ludgate Hill and Cornhill. The higher of the two was believed to be Ludgate Hill, where St Paul's Cathedral now stands, although surveying techniques have proved that Cornhill is the higher by about 12 inches.

An alternative name for a bread basket is a panyer, and more than three centuries ago, the plaque was originally on a wall in Panyer Alley, named after a nearby inn called The Panyer, which burned down in the Great Fire of London.

The Panyer Boy plaque, which claims to mark the highest point in London.

The boy on the plaque is naked, indicative, some say, of the fact that bread boys in days gone by were extremely badly paid.

* * *

London's Only Nazi Monument

Given the circumstances of the Second World War, it would seem highly unlikely that London should harbour a Nazi monument. But it does, although it's not a monument to a man or woman. It's in the form of a small grave and it's in honour of a dog.

The grave can be seen in front of a tree behind the gates of 9 Carlton Terrace, today an imposing white building not far from Buckingham Palace and St James's Park.

The reason it's there goes back to 1934, five years before the outbreak of the Second World War, when the building housed the

German Embassy. The dog's name was Giro and he was owned by the German Ambassador Leopold von Hoesch.

Although von Hoesch was believed not to be a dedicated Nazi supporter, he was appointed to serve Hitler's regime a year after his arrival in London when the Nazi party sized power in Germany in 1933.

The Ambassador might not have been devoted to Hitler, but he was devoted to Giro. When Giro died in 1934, after being electrocuted by an exposed wire, von Hoesch had him

Giro's grave, behind the gates in Carlton House Terrace.

buried in the grounds of the Embassy, where a small tombstone was erected in his honour. It's still there today, and reads, in German, '*Ein Treuer Begleiter!*', which translates as 'A Faithful Companion!' Leopold von Hoesch died two years later in 1936, three years before the outbreak of the Second World War.

* * *

The Deformed Maidens of St Pancras

There's something not quite right about four stone figures used as part of the architecture of St Pancras New Church in Euston Road. The figures are correctly known as caryatids, the term for sculpted female figures used as an architectural support in place of columns. In this case they support the flat roof of an alcove, hidden away at the back of the church.

At first sight they look conventional enough, but closer examination reveals that they are just slightly deformed. The reason is that they were made slightly too tall to fit the space prepared for them during the building of the church between 1819 and 1822.

The slightly deformed maidens that support part of St Pancras New Church.

The figures were made from Coade's artificial stone, whose exact formula is no longer known, and took three years to make. But when they arrived on site, they were found to be too tall. So the builder removed about 12 inches from the middle of each of the figures. Hence the reason why today, they appear a little less lithe than was the original intention.

* * *

The London Tomb of a German Philospher

It comes as a shock to some to learn that the famous German philosopher and revolutionary communist Karl Marx was buried in a London cemetery. When you learn something of his history, it is less surprising.

Marx was a hugely influential philosopher who was born in Germany in 1818, where he studied law and received a doctorate in philosophy. Moving to Paris, he befriended fellow German philosopher, social scientist and journalist Friedrich Engels and became a communist. Expelled from France, he moved on to Brussels, where he and Engels co-authored *The*

Communist Manifesto, published in 1848. The next year he moved to London, were he wrote *Das Kapital*, known as the bible of the working class. He died in 1883 and was buried in Highgate Cemetery.

The grave of Karl Marx, in Highgate Cemetery.

Although Marx lived much of his time in London in poverty, his more affluent friend Engels financed the grave in Highgate Cemetery. He was initially buried with his wife who had died in 1881, and whom he deeply mourned. In 1954, his remains were moved to a new, better position, and the impressive tomb that resides here now was commissioned by the Communist Party of Great Britain. It was designed by Laurence Bradshaw, an English sculptor, printmaker and artist, who was also a member of the Party.

The impressive tomb comprises a tall granite slab with a huge bronze head of Marx on top. Set in gold at the top of the slab are the words 'Workers of all lands unite.' At the base are the words 'The philosophers have only interpreted the world in various ways – the point however is to change it.'

* * *

The Man Who Defeated the Great Stink

Close to Hungerford Bridge, on the north bank of the river Thames, there is a memorial to a man with the unusual name of Sir Joseph Bazalgette. Compared to most memorials, this one is relatively small, and embedded as it is into the river's embankment wall, it's easy to miss.

Although small, the memorial is ornate, with stone pillars each side of a bronze bust of Bazalgette, a small pitched roof above it and an ornamental plinth below. The inscriptions on the memorial give clues to why Bazalgette was so important to London.

The one above his bust, in Latin, states '*Flumini vincula posvit*', which translates as 'He put the river in chains.' The one below goes some way towards explaining this somewhat enigmatic epitaph: 'Sir Joseph Bazalgette, CB. Engineer of the London main drainage system and of this embankment. Born 1819. Died 1891.'

As Chief Engineer of the London Metropolitan Board of Works, Sir Joseph Bazalgette was the man who devised a new sewage system for London, a project that began in 1859 and took nine years

Memorial to Sir Joseph Bazalgette, who designed the London sewage system.

to complete. At the time, it was the biggest civil engineering project in the world.

It has been estimated that the 2.5 million people who lived in mid-nineteenth-century London produced many million gallons of sewage and general filth each day. The waste was carried in open drains that sloped down to the Thames to be dumped straight into the river. The streets smelled vile and the river was little more than an open sewer. Things came to a head in the hot summer of 1858, when a combination of the heat and the heavily polluted Thames resulted in Members of Parliament being forced to hang sacking soaked with deodorising chemicals at the windows of the House of Commons that bordered the Thames at Westminster.

It became known as the year of The Great Stink, prompting the government to rush a bill through Parliament to provide the money to construct an ambitious sewer system for London. The bill became law in eighteen days and Bazalgette took on the task of designing a system that, by means of both gravity and pumping stations along the way, diverted the waste to two locations in the Thames Estuary, about 14 miles east of London Bridge and at a suitable distance from the main population of London.

In so doing, he also built new embankments along the Thames, which pushed the river back about 100 yards from its original course. That's why his memorial refers to him as the man who put the river in chains – and it's how he defeated The Great Stink.

* * *

Where to Sit and Chat with Oscar Wilde

Oscar Wilde is recognised as one of the English language's greatest playwrights. But although he died in 1900, no significant memorial to him was unveiled in London until nearly 100 years after his death.

The memorial is located in Adelaide Street, close to Charing Cross station. It was designed by British painter and sculptor Maggi Hambling. She was one of twelve artists invited to submit designs to a committee of actors and artists who came together to honour the playwright. Funds for the project were raised by public subscription.

The memorial to Oscar Wilde, in Adelaide Street.

The memorial takes the form of a green granite sarcophagus with a bronze head of the great man rising from his tomb, and seeming to be in the middle of a conversation. On one end of the memorial a quotation from *Lady Windermere's Fan*, one of his best-known plays, is inscribed, stating: 'We are all in the gutter but some of us are looking at the stars.'

The sarcophagus is vaguely coffin-shaped and doubles as a bench on which members of the public are welcome to sit and chat with the great man. It's why the official title given to the memorial is *A Conversation with Oscar Wilde.*

The memorial was unveiled in 1998 by comedian, actor, writer, presenter and activist Stephen Fry.

* * *

Sit on a Seat with Churchill and Roosevelt

At the point where New Bond street meets Old Bond Street in Mayfair, bronze statues of two renowned world leaders, who were last united during the years of the Second World War, sit chatting like a couple of old friends on a wooden bench. They are British Prime Minister Winston Churchill and American President Franklin Roosevelt.

Churchill and Roosevelt share a seat in Mayfair.

The two statesmen were largely responsible for implementing the Atlantic Charter, which set goals for peace in the post-war world. The strong bond between the two men was a major factor in forging the transatlantic partnership between the two countries that endures today.

Posed on the bench at the junction of the two Bond Streets, the full size, life-like statues, are seated with a space between them that many a passing person has sat on for a quick photo opportunity. The monument, called *Allies*, was unveiled in 1995 to mark fifty years of peace, following the anniversary of the end of the Second World War in 1945.

The sculpture is by the American Lawrence Holofcener, whose statues of famous people have been exhibited across the US and the UK. A copy of the sculpture sold in the UK in 2012 for £409,250.

* * *

A Memorial to Exploding Traffic Lights

London is full of plaques on buildings celebrating and commemorating the lives and discoveries of a vast range of people and personalities. Most plaques are easy to see and celebrate success. The one on a building in Bridge Street right opposite the Houses of Parliament is harder to find, since it is positioned high up. Also it celebrates something that, despite being a good idea at the time, was actually something of a failure.

Memorial plaque at Westminster dedicated to the man who invented the first traffic lights.

The inventor commemorated on the plaque is engineer and railway manager John Peake Knight, who specialised in designing signalling systems for the railway network, which grew at a fast pace in Victorian times. He was also credited with being one of the first to introduce emergency brake cords into railway carriages.

Although there were no cars on the road at the time, the growing use of horse-drawn vehicles was becoming a danger to pedestrians and Knight saw a need for introducing some kind of traffic control. In 1865, he came up with an idea to control London traffic by means of a signalling system similar to that used on railways.

As a result, three years later, in 1868, the world's first traffic lights were erected in Westminster. They took the form of twin semaphore-like arms – straight out meant stop, both pointing down meant caution – with red and green gas lamps above, operated manually by a policeman. The signals cum traffic lights were immediately successful, but not for long. A month after the lights were erected, a gas leak caused them to explode, seriously injuring the policeman. Deemed too dangerous to remain, the lights were removed.

Traffic lights did not become commonplace in London until 1929, when the first electric versions were introduced.

The plaque in Westminster reads: 'John Peak Knight 1828–86. Inventor of the world's first traffic lights which were erected here in December 1868.' It was unveiled in 1998.

* * *

Doctor Johnson's Cat

Outside a house in Gough Square there stands a bronze statue of a cat. But this isn't just any cat. It's Doctor Johnson's cat.

Samuel Johnson, most often referred to as Doctor Johnson, was a lexicographer, who wrote what became the most influential dictionary in the English language. His wasn't the first or only dictionary, but it was the best, having been written at the request of a group London booksellers. He began the work in 1746 and it was published nine years later in 1755. Johnson's fee for writing

Dr Johnson's cat, outside his house in Gough Square.

the dictionary was the amazing sum of 1,500 guineas, or £1,575, a truly huge sum of money for that time. It was called *A Dictionary of the English Language* and remained the paramount work of its type for 173 years, when the *Oxford English Dictionary* was completed.

Johnson has also gone down in history as an eminent writer, poet, essayist, literary critic and editor. Less known is his love for his cats, and one in particular. His name was Hodge, who was often mentioned in Johnson's essays and poems. He was fed on oysters, which, unlike today, were plentiful and inexpensive in the eighteenth century. When Hodge died, Johnson's neighbour, the poet Percival Stockdale, celebrated the cat's life in a poem called *An Elegy on The Death of Dr Johnson's Favourite Cat*.

Johnson lived at 17 Gough Square. Today, the house is a museum, where you can see the garret where the great man's dictionary was written, relax in his library and discover much about his life. The memorial to Hodge stands outside the house.

The bronze statue of Doctor Johnson's cat is sitting on a copy of his master's dictionary, next to a couple of oyster shells. The sculptor was Jon Bickley, an exponent of works of art based on animals. Not knowing exactly what Hodge looked like, Bickley modelled him on his own cat. The memorial was unveiled by the Lord Mayor of the City of London in 1997.

* * *

Animals in War Memorial

War memorials can be seen throughout the UK, and London obviously has its fair share. Most are dedicated to members of the armed forces who gave their lives in various wars. But one, just outside Hyde Park where Park Lane meets Upper Brook Street, is there in honour all the animals that served, suffered and died alongside British, Allied and Commonwealth forces in the many conflicts of the twentieth century.

The memorial takes the form of a curved wall displaying carvings of animals. Bronze mules, one weighed down with cartwheels, struggle through a gap in one side of the wall, while a horse and dog emerge from the other side. Under the main inscription detailing the dedication to the animals is a smaller, more poignant message that simply reads: 'They had no choice.'

The part played by animals in warfare is celebrated close to Hyde Park.

The memorial was designed by sculptor David Backhouse. It was unveiled by the Princess Royal in 2004.

* * *

Albert's Two Memorials

On the edge of Kensington Gardens, opposite the Royal Albert Hall, there stands one of the most ornate and possibly the most ostentatious monument in London. Its reason for being there isn't what many believe.

The Albert Memorial

The popular belief is that the Albert Memorial was erected in honour of Prince Albert's work in the organisation of The Great Exhibition of 1851, which was designed to show off the country's expertise to the world, and for the world to come to Britain to show what other countries also had to offer and to boast about.

Prince Albert, who was husband and Consort to Queen Victoria, was a major player in the success of the exhibition, but the fact that he is seen in the centre of the memorial with the exhibition

The Albert Memorial, at the edge of Kensington Gardens.

catalogue on his knee is the only tangible connection with The Great Exhibition. The Albert Memorial was in fact erected, at the instigation of Queen Victoria, simply to honour the memory of the man to whom she was devoted, and whose death caused her to wear black until her own death, forty years after Albert died of typhoid in 1861.

At Queen Victoria's request, work began on the memorial in 1862. It was designed by English architect Sir George Gilbert Scott, reflecting his interest in the Gothic Revival style. Work began in 1864 and the monument was unveiled in 1872 – without Albert's statue in the centre. It was another three years before that was put in place. Its creator was Irish sculptor John Henry Foley, who took over after the death of Italian-born French sculptor Carlo Marochetti, whose design was deemed unsatisfactory anyway.

Beautifully restored in the 1990s, the Albert Memorial stands 176 feet high, with the gilt bronze statue of Prince Albert, robed as a Knight of the Garter, sitting at its centre, surrounded at the base by sculptures that represent Europe, Asia, Africa and the Americas. From here, flights of stone steps rise on each side to a platform where four more statues, one at each corner, represent Victorian arts and sciences: agriculture, commerce, engineering and manufactures. An elaborate frieze that shows 169 famous figures surrounds the central part of the memorial, and above Albert, there is a canopy featuring mosaics, representing poetry, painting, architecture and sculpture. More statues stand near the top of the canopy's tower to depict moral and Christian values:

faith, hope, charity, humility, fortitude, prudence, justice and temperance. Above these, gilded angels raise their arms to the sky and a gold cross stands at the pinnacle of the memorial.

It's difficult to image what more could possibly have been added to such a flamboyant and grandiose memorial to the life of one man.

Albert's other memorial

The Prince's work for The Great Exhibition is celebrated in another memorial, a short distance away. To find it you need to cross Kensington Gore,

Albert's other memorial, at the back of the Royal Albert Hall.

the road that runs between the Albert Memorial and the Royal Albert Hall, and walk round the huge circular concert hall to the opposite side.

Here you'll find a more modest, but nevertheless still impressive monument depicting Albert atop a tall plinth with, seated at its base, four figures that represent Europe, America, Asia and Africa, echoing similar, but rather more complex, statues on the Albert Memorial across the road.

Commissioned from sculptor Joseph Durham, the original intention was to commemorate the exhibition with a figure of Britannia as the centrepiece of the monument. But after Prince Albert's death in 1861, the decision was made to put Albert in place of the female embodiment of all that is British.

The monument was first erected in the gardens of the Royal Horticultural Society at Kensington in 1863. In 1890, it was moved to its new site behind the Royal Albert Hall, where it remains today, somewhat in the shadow of the Albert Memorial nearby, but nevertheless as a lasting tribute to Prince Albert and his vision of The Great Exhibition.

* * *

Eighteenth-Century School Uniforms

If you have ever wondered how schoolchildren dressed in the eighteenth century, you need look no further than the side of a building in St Marychurch Street, South London. This is St Mary's Free School, founded in 1613 by two Elizabethan mariners, Peter Hill and Robert Bell, for the education of the children of local seafarers.

The school was instituted as a charity establishment in 1742, and was moved to its present location in 1797 from its original position next to nearby St Mary's Church. It is thought to be the oldest elementary school in London. A memorial plaque in the church identifies one of the school's founders, Peter Hills, as 'Mariner, one of the Elder Brothers of the Company of the Trinity and Master of Trinity House in 1593.'

STMARY ROTHERHITHE
FREE SCHOOL Founded by PETER HILL and ESQ⁹ 1613 ROBERT BELL
CHARITY SCHOOL instituted   1742
Removed here   1797
Supported by Voluntary Contributions

Statues outside St Mary's Free School show how pupils dressed in the eighteenth century.

Above the entrance to the building, on either side of a first-floor window, stand two statues of a boy and girl wearing the traditional blue coats of charity schoolchildren. The school provided education for local children until 1939.

The smaller building to the side of the school, now a café, was once a watch house, used in the nineteenth century by constables or watchmen looking out for body snatchers who robbed graves in the adjacent cemetery in order to sell the bodies to medical students.

* * *

The Monument

Probably the most obvious of London's more famous monuments is the one simply called The Monument. It's well known that it is a memorial to the Great Fire of London. But it's more than that.

How The Monument looked soon after it was built in 1677.

The Monument stands at the junction of Fish Street Hill and Monument Street, close to the northern end of London Bridge. It was built to commemorate the Great Fire of London, which raged for three days in 1666, destroying almost everything in its path within the old Roman city wall and decimating 436 acres containing more than 13,000 houses, nearly ninety churches and the original St Paul's Cathedral. The Monument was designed by acclaimed English architect Christopher Wren, who, among his many notable achievements, also designed the present St Paul's Cathedral. For The Monument, he worked with English philosopher and architect Robert Hook. It was built between 1671 and 1677 and consists of a Doric column, 202 feet tall with a gilded urn of fire at the top. Its height is the distance between its base and the spot in nearby Pudding Lane, where the fire started in a bakery.

The column is hollow. Inside, 311 steps wind in a spiral staircase up to a platform close to the top, from where visitors can take in magnificent panoramic views of London.

The base on which the column stands is inscribed on three sides in Latin. One side describes the actions taken by King Charles II after the fire. The inscription on an adjacent panel describes how The Monument was conceived and built. A third panel speaks of how the fire started and the damage it caused. Further words blaming Catholics for the fire were chiselled out in 1830. The fourth side of the base contains a bas-relief sculpture illustrating the destruction caused by the fire, with King Charles and his brother James giving direction for the restoration.

What is not so often recorded is that The Monument was originally built to serve two functions: not just as a memorial to the Great Fire but also as a scientific instrument. For this latter purpose it was built to house a zenith telescope – one made to point straight up – that looked up the central shaft of the hollow column and out of a hinged lid in the ornamental urn at the top of the structure. With this, Wren and Hook planned to observe the movement of the Earth around the Sun over a long period of time.

The two architects also built an underground laboratory directly beneath the spiral staircase, from where they could conduct experiments with gravity and the differences in barometric pressure

The Monument today.

The spiral staircase, from the top, looking down.

The bas-relief sculpture on the base of The Monument.

between the base and the top of the column. Sadly, the weight and vibrations of traffic in the surrounding streets put paid to much of the scientific experimentation planned by the two visionaries.

Today, you can climb the staircase to emerge on the platform beneath the gilded urn at the top. The underground laboratory is still there, but sealed off from the public.

* * *

The Golden Boy of Pie Corner

The Great Fire of London started in Pudding Lane, and strangely, ended at Pye Corner, where there is another monument, though not as impressive as The Monument that officially commemorates the fire and is positioned close to its start. The monument at its end takes the form of a small golden statue, originally known as The Fat Boy when it was put in place in the seventeenth century. In the 1800s, it was gilded and its name changed to The Golden Boy.

The small statue originally sat in a recess in the walls of a pub called The Fortune of War, which stood at the point where Cock Lane meets Giltspur Street. In the 1800s, the

The Golden Boy of Pie Corner marks the point where the Great Fire of London stopped.

pub was much used by grave robbers who stashed their stolen corpses in a back room until they were picked up by surgeons at nearby St Bartholomew's Hospital.

The pub was demolished in 1910, but The Golden Boy statue survived and still stands today in a small niche in the present building.

Its original purpose was twofold: to mark where the fire stopped and to warn that, since the fire started in Pudding Lane and ended at Pye (or pie) Corner, it had been caused by greedy Londoners.

It is worth mentioning, perhaps, that the word pudding at that time didn't refer to a delicious desert in the way it does today. In seventeenth-century London, pudding was a term for animal guts and Pudding Lane was home to many butchers, who tossed animal waste into the streets where it was washed down to the river Thames. Even so, the inscription below The Golden Boy of Pye Corner state states: *'This Boy is in Memory put up for the late Fire of London, occasion'd by the Sin of Gluttony.'*

* * *

The Temple Bar Griffin

At the point where the Strand runs into Fleet Street, outside the London Law Courts, there stands a remarkable granite monument, comprising a richly ornamented tower, incorporating statues of Queen Victoria and the Prince of Wales, all topped by a mighty dragon.

The monument was designed by Sir Horace Jones, architect and surveyor to the City of London, who is best known for the design concept behind Tower Bridge. It has stood on this spot since 1878, when it replaced the Temple Bar Gate, the principal ceremonial entrance to the City of London from the City of Westminster.

The dragon is the symbol of the City of London and appears on the City arms, along with the Cross of St George.

The Temple Bar griffin, which stands outside London's Law Courts.

Traditionally such beasts stood as boundary markers and guardians of the borders of the City. Over the years, this particular dragon has become better known as a griffin, a legendary beast that is half lion and half eagle.

The sculptures of Queen Victoria on one side of the plinth and of the Prince of Wales on the opposite side are there to commemorate the fact that these were the last members of the Royal Family to pass through the old gate before it was relocated. Among other sculptures and reliefs, the plinth displays emblems of war and peace, alongside symbols of human endeavour that include the arts, sciences and navigation in tribute to Victorian achievements, of which there were many.

* * *

Nelson's Misshapen Lions

Nelson's Column in Trafalgar Square isn't exactly hidden away. It's among the most prominent monuments in London. But it isn't all it seems.

The column was designed by English architect William Railton, built from Dartmoor granite in the Corinthian style and cost £47,000. The statue of Nelson that stands at its top is more than 18 feet tall, made from sandstone and was the work of English sculptor Edward Hodges Baily. At the base of the column four relief panels depict Nelson's most famous battles. The panels are made of bronze, cast from captured French guns.

The memorial is in honour of Admiral Horatio Nelson, who died at the Battle of Trafalgar in 1805. Although the British wanted to commemorate his achievements as soon as possible, money was short due to the ongoing Napoleonic Wars, and it was thirty-eight years before the column was completed in 1843 – and then the height was wrongly recorded.

Nelson's Column, in Trafalgar Square.

The relief panels that depict Nelson's battles, made of bronze from captured French guns.

One of Landseer's lions, with its slightly misshapen back.

It was believed that the monument was 185 feet high. But during a cleaning operation in 2006, it was discovered that it is actually 16 feet shorter.

There is also something wrong with the lions that stand at the base of Nelson's Column. These were not installed until 1867, twenty-four years after the column was completed and sixty-two years after Nelson's death. The lions were designed by Sir Edwin Landseer, who was famous for his paintings of animals, particularly dogs and stags. Unfortunately, when it came to lions, it seems he wasn't so well informed. Lions, when they lie down, do so with their backs slightly arched. Landseer designed his lions with concave backs.

Although anatomically wrong, the result makes the lions more comfortable for the many tourists who regularly climb on them and sit on their backs.

* * *

Where the *Mayflower* Really Sailed From

It is well documented that when the Pilgrim Fathers left England, bound for the New World in 1620, they sailed on the *Mayflower* and, after a couple of false starts, finally left from Plymouth in Devon. So why are there so many memorials and references to the ship, its captain and the journey at Rotherhithe in South London?

A plaque on the wall of a church in Rotherhithe celebrates the start of the *Mayflower's* epic voyage.

The truth is that although the *Mayflower* has become linked with Plymouth, its origins came from nowhere near the Devon town. The *Mayflower* was built in Essex and first registered at Harwich, a town in the north-east of the county, more than 300 miles from Plymouth. Harwich was also the birthplace and home of Christopher Jones, the ship's captain, where he and three other business partners purchased the ship, initially to be used as a trading vessel.

In 1611, Jones moved to Rotherhithe, and it was from here that the *Mayflower* actually set sail on the first leg of its famous journey.

Taking on crew and some passengers from South London, it sailed along the river to the open sea, then to the south coast of England, where it took on more passengers and officially began its epic voyage from Southampton. It was accompanied by a sister ship called the *Speedwell*, which had brought more emigrants for the trip from the Netherlands. Unfortunately, the *Speedwell* soon began to leak, forcing the two ships to return to Dartmouth for repairs, before setting off again. About 300 miles out to sea, the *Speedwell* again began to leak, so this time they returned to Plymouth. Here, the *Speedwell's* passengers and cargo were transferred to the *Mayflower*, which then set sail for the New World alone.

That's why Plymouth gets the glory, and also why Rotherhithe is full of memorials to Captain Jones and his ship.

In Rotherhithe Street there is a pub called the Mayflower, and on its roof, a model of the famous ship is built into the weather vane. The pub, which dates back to the 1550s, has only been known as the Mayflower since 1957. Before that it was called the Spread Eagle and Crown. But back in 1620, it was an inn, known as The Shippe. This is where the *Mayflower* began its journey, leaving from the inn's landing steps.

The same inn was also once a riverside Post Office, and so today lays claim to being the only place in London licensed to sell both British and American postage stamps.

Close to the Mayflower pub, the present church of St Mary the Virgin was built in 1716 to replace a medieval church that stood on the same spot. A plaque on the wall of the tower states: 'In 1620 the *Mayflower* sailed from Rotherhithe on the first stage of its epic voyage to America. In command was

The Mayflower pub, formerly known at the Ship Inn, from where the *Mayflower* set sail.

Captain Christopher Jones of Rotherhithe.' Christopher Jones's children were baptised in the church that previously stood on this spot, and he was buried in the churchyard in 1622, not long after his return from America. Two of his business partners are also buried in the churchyard. The exact location of the graves is unknown today, but a memorial tablet inside the church celebrates their lives and achievements.

The weather vane on the roof of the Mayflower pub is in the shape of the famous ship.

In the current churchyard, a memorial unveiled in 1995 shows Captain Jones holding a small child. He is depicted looking back towards England, whilst the child is looking forward towards America. The statue is by designer and public art sculptor Jamie Sargeant.

Rotherhithe's final memorial to the voyage of the *Mayflower* is perhaps the most curious. It's a statue, standing at Cumberland Wharf, depicting a Pilgrim and a small boy. Although it's pretty much certain today that the Pilgrims didn't wear the smocks and tall hats with which they have become habitually associated, that's the way the Pilgrim statue is dressed. The boy is dressed in the style of a 1930s' newsboy. He is reading a newspaper, called the *Sunshine*

The memorial to Christopher Jones in the local churchyard.

Weekly, whose sculpted pages tell the story of the *Mayflower* and all that has happened in America since its voyage.

One page shows the voyage in a comic strip; the other shows images of America through the ages since the voyage: a cowboy, the Statue of Liberty, the Empire State Building, American cars, a US soldier and more. The Pilgrim is standing ghost-like, reading the paper and pointing to a page over the boy's shoulder, while a small dog leaps around their feet.

In a further anachronism, the Pilgrim's pocket contains a copy of the A-Z street map of London, which, despite not coming into being until the 1930s, is dated 1620

A Pilgrim Father and a small boy form a life-size statue at Cumberland Wharf.

– the date of the Pilgrim Fathers' voyage. His pocket also contains a crucifix and a lobster's claw, while various tools – scissors, hammer, pliers and a paintbrush – are shown at the boy's feet.

The statue was commissioned in 1991. Called *Sunshine Weekly and the Pilgrim's Pocket*, it was produced by sculptor Peter McClean.

Because it was the last point of embarkation, and the last dry land seen by the Pilgrim Fathers before their voyage, Plymouth has become inextricably linked with the journey. (In fact, the place they landed, coincidentally, had already been named New Plymouth by soldier and explorer John Smith a few years before.) But the truth is that Harwich to some small extent, and Rotherhithe to a larger extent, has far stronger connections with the voyage often hailed as the one that began the colonisation of America.

Chapter 12

Lost Locations

Across London you'll find examples of large, ornate and often ostentatious gateways that lead nowhere – places that are now lost forever. Likewise, it's easy to stumble across locations that look conventionally ordinary today, but which have strange and forgotten pasts. Here are a few examples.

* * *

Marble Arch

In 1827, British architect John Nash, who was responsible for much of the layout of Regency London, designed a huge arch made of high quality Carrara marble. The design was based on the triumphal Arch

Marble Arch, when it stood at the entrance to Buckingham Palace.

of Constantine built in Rome in the fourth century. The purpose of the London version was to form a grand gateway to Buckingham Palace. So why does the arch stand today on a site 2 miles from the palace, marking the entrance to nowhere?

The fact is that it did once stand at the entrance to Buckingham Palace, but it was moved at the request of Queen Victoria. The common belief is that its removal was part of plans to enlarge the palace to accommodate the expanding Royal Family. An alternative claim that it was too narrow for the state coach to pass through was negated when the coach passed through it on the occasion of the Coronation of Queen Elizabeth II in June 1953.

A bronze statue of King George IV on horseback was planned to sit on top of the arch when it was positioned outside Buckingham Palace, but when the King died, the statue was placed instead in Trafalgar Square.

Marble Arch, where it stands today.

Work began on the arch's careful demolition in 1847, and it was reopened at its new location in 1851 as a grand entrance to Hyde Park. Today the edge of the park is some distance away from the arch, which is stranded in the middle of a busy traffic system, due to the widening of Park Lane in the 1950s.

Carvings in the marble depict figures that represent England, Scotland and Wales. Other carvings indicate peace and plenty, while another shows a naval warrior holding the figure of justice. Embedded in the arch's bronze gates are the lion of England, and the country's patron saint, St George, with the dragon that legend has it he slew.

In the top of the arch, three small rooms were once used as a police station and by police to keep watch over the surrounding area, most notably in 1855, when a demonstration by a rioting crowd was quickly suppressed by the surprising emergence of police officers from the arch.

Marble Arch stands today on the site of the old Tyburn Tree gallows, where, for many years, thousands of robbers, murderers, highwaymen, traitors and other criminals were hanged, until the last culprit met his fate here in 1783.

* * *

Wellington Arch

About a mile from Marble Arch along Park Lane at Hyde Park Corner there is another impressive gateway isolated in the middle of a traffic roundabout. This is the Wellington Arch, planned in 1825 by King George IV to celebrate Britain's victories in the Napoleonic Wars. It was designed by English architect and garden designer Decimus Burton.

The Wellington Arch's original location was at the top of Constitution Hill, where it formed an outer entrance to Buckingham Palace. A statue of the Duke of Wellington was placed on top in 1846, but a road widening scheme in 1882 caused the arch to be moved to its present position, when the statue of Wellington was removed. It was

Wellington Arch, in the centre of Hyde Park Corner.

replaced in 1912 with a statue of the Angel of Peace in a chariot drawn by four horses that is still there today. It is the largest bronze sculpture in Europe. Further road widening in the 1960s has left the arch in the middle of the large traffic island.

Wellington Arch, originally called the Green Park Arch and also known as Constitution Arch, is hollow. Like the nearby Marble Arch, it was used as a police station until 1992. It is now open to the public, where exhibits are on display detailing the arch's history. Terraces on each side give views of the surrounding area, including Buckingham Palace Gardens, the Royal Parks and the Houses of Parliament.

Part of the arch also acts as a ventilation system for the underpass at Hyde Park Corner. So if you see what appears to be smoke rising from the arch, don't worry. You won't be the first to think Wellington Arch is on fire. It's just warm air and dust arising from the underpass.

* * *

York Watergate

In Embankment Gardens between Waterloo and Hungerford bridges on the north bank of the river Thames there stands a large and very ornate gateway that leads to nothing at all. It dates back to a time when a long row of mansions ran along Strand (more commonly known as The Strand), whose name actually means 'river shore'.

York House was one of the great houses, built in the thirteenth century and gaining its name when it was granted to the Bishop of York in 1556. Later, among many other owners, it was acquired by George Villiers, the First Duke of Buckingham and a favourite of King James I.

Like other mansions along this row, the garden of York House extended down to the Thames, giving easy access to the river. In 1826, George Villiers extended York House and had the gate built by English architect Inigo Jones. Down through the years it has been variously known as the Buckingham Watergate, York Watergate and The York Stairs.

The gateway comprises three carved stone archways with a curved arch above the central one complete with a coat of arms inscribed 'Fidei cotucula crux', which translates as 'the cross is the touchstone of faith'. That was the motto of the Villiers family, whose name lives on in the name of nearby Villiers Street.

The York Watergate, in Embankment Gardens.

In 1859, work began on a new sewage system for London, involving the building of the Victoria Embankment, which in turn pushed the banks of the river back more than 100 yards. Then York House was demolished in 1865. Only the gateway, which originally led to York House on the northern side, with the river lapping against its steps on the southern side, remains today, standing in splendid isolation, at the edge of Embankment Gardens.

* * *

Barking's Bell Gate Tower

The London Borough of Barking and Dagenham was one of the new boroughs created in 1965. Before that, Barking was in the county of Essex, and despite appearing to be an unexceptional East London conurbation today, the town actually has a lot of history behind it. Much of it has now disappeared, but one important landmark remains in the shape of the Bell Gate Tower.

Today it stands alone, close to busy roads and a modern shopping centre. But once it marked one of

The Bell Gate Tower, in Barking.

The folly that purports to be part of the Abbey ruins was actually built in 2007.

three entrances to Barking Abbey, established in the seventh century and reckoned to be one of the most important nunneries in Britain. The abbey functioned for about 900 years until 1539, when it was closed by King Henry VIII's Dissolution of the Monasteries. The abbey was demolished in 1541, and all that remains of the building is the outline of its footings in nearby parkland called Abbey Green.

The Bell Gate Tower, also known as the Curfew Tower, however, is still standing, and it is Grade II listed. Originally built in 1370 and then rebuilt a century later, it has been repaired and restored many times since. It takes its name from an ancient custom enforced by William I, which decreed that people should extinguish and relight all fires and candles at certain hours of the day. A bell tolled from the tower to indicate when this should take place. Today the Tower forms an entrance to the churchyard of St Margaret's Church, originally built as a chapel within the grounds of the abbey.

Don't be fooled by a nearby high wall and bricked-up entrance that purport to be an important part of the abbey ruins. This is actually a folly, built by apprentice bricklayers in 2007, using old bricks, to recreate a fragment of Barking's lost history.

* * *

Temple Bar

At the entrance to Paternoster Square, close to St Paul's Cathedral, there stands a huge and ancient gateway that seems somewhat out of place among the modern office blocks and shops beyond. It's not surprising. The Square was built in the 1960s, following heavy bombing of the area during the Second World War. The gateway dates back to the fourteenth century, and was originally erected a little under a mile away from its present location.

The gateway is called the Temple Bar, and at the time it was built, this was one of the original gateways to the City of London, of which there were eight. It is the only one that still survives. Reputed to have been designed by Sir Christopher Wren, the architect of St Paul's

The Temple Bar as it looked when it stood as an entrance to the City of London.

Cathedral, it survived the Great Fire of London, and in the eighteenth century, it was one of the places in London where the heads of traitors were displayed on iron spikes.

The gate stood at the junction of Fleet Street and the Strand for two centuries before it was demolished in 1878 to allow for road widening. Rather than completely destroying it, however, it was taken apart stone by stone, each one numbered and put into storage.

The last resting place for the Temple Bar.

Ten years later, it came to the attention of wealthy socialite Valerie, Lady Meux, the wife of London brewer Sir Henry Meux. Looking for a way to impress her friends and acquaintances, she had the parts transported to her estate at Theobald's Park in Hertfordshire, where the gateway was rebuilt.

There it remained until the Temple Bar Trust was established with a view to bringing the gateway back to London. In 2001, the Corporation of London agreed to fund the cost of its removal, and the old Temple Bar was once more moved brick by brick, to be built for a third time at its present location. It was officially reopened by the Lord Mayor of London in 2004.

* * *

Tothill Fields Prison Gate

Across the road from Westminster Abbey, in Little George Street, there is a building whose entrance is surrounded by a stone gateway that looks out of place. The reason the building and the gateway do not appear to belong together is because the gateway was originally the prison gate for the Tothill Fields House of Correction, which stood where Westminster Cathedral now stands.

The prison, which was known to be more humane than most of its time, was one of many established as places for the punishment and reform of the poor who had been convicted of petty offences. Punishment was in the form of

The gateway to Tothill Fields House of Correction, still standing in Little George Street.

hard labour. The prison stood on this site from 1618 to 1884, when the land was purchased as the site for Westminster Cathedral, which still stands on the site as the mother church for the Catholic faith in England and Wales.

The gateway, which is all that remains of the old prison, survived the building's demolition and was placed at its present location in 1959.

* * *

Cockpit Steps

Birdcage Walk runs from the junction of Great George Street and Horse Guards Road, near the north side of Westminster Bridge, to Buckingham Gate, close to Buckingham Palace. Halfway along, on the side of the road opposite St James's Park, there is the narrow entrance to a stone stairway called Cockpit Steps, which leads down to Old Queen Street. This Grade II listed location is so called because it is all that remains of the Old Royal Cockpit.

The entrance to what was one of London's most prestigious cock-fighting pits.

Here, in the eighteenth century, the wealthy upper classes met to watch and bet on cock fights. Cock fighting was a popular pastime dating back to the Tudor era, in the late fifteenth century. It was not only legal, but very well regulated. Its rules were extremely complex and whole books were written on the subject.

The Royal Cockpit was one of the better venues, favoured by the rich, as is evidenced by the fact that the admission charge in the eighteenth century would have been something like five shillings (25p and worth about £50 today). It was more usual for cockpits to be less expensive, but noisy, dirty and disorderly places frequented by the lower classes. Cock fighting was outlawed in 1835.

Stories that Cockpit Steps retained its name from its proximity to a number of Victorian brothels are largely unfounded.

* * *

Pickering Place

Pickering Place, off of St James's Street, is the smallest public square in London. It is also the place where bear-baiting once took place; where Napoleon III, exiled in London for ten years from 1838, planned his return to France; and where London's last duel was fought.

Today, Pickering Place is reached through a narrow, oak-panelled alley next to No. 3 St James's Street. The alley opens onto the tiny paved square, which is characterised by Georgian architecture, a sundial and ancient gas lamps. The bear-baiting that took place here was a barbaric sport in which a bear was tied to a post and set upon by fierce dogs.

It is thought that the last duel was fought with swords, though the identity of the duellists is unclear today.

Pickering Place, where London's last duel was fought.

Chapter 13

Roman Remains

London was established by the Romans in the middle of the first century. The location they chose was a plot of land on a river they called the Thamesis, later known as the Thames. The Romans called their new settlement Londinium, the exact etymology of which is unknown. One theory suggests that it was derived from the Celtic word Londinion, which was the name of a local chieftain. Another, more complicated, explanation is that it was adapted from an existing pre-Celtic name that was something like Plowonida from two words suggesting a wide, flowing river. This, in turn, became Lowonidonjon in Celtic times, Londinium in the Roman era, and finally, London.

None of these theories can be substantially proven. What is certain is that the river at this location was narrow enough that it could be easily bridged, extending and enhancing communications between the north and the south of the country. The river was also tidal at this point, which meant it was deep enough for ships to come in from the coast, making the location ideal as a trading post.

Londinium grew and prospered until AD 60, when Queen Boudica, leading a revolt against Roman rule, attacked the city while the Roman army was mostly occupied quelling an uprising in Wales. As a result the whole city was burnt to the ground. The Romans, however, quickly established rule again and rebuilt the city. Londinium flourished and became a major centre of trade.

More than 2,000 years later, there are still remains of the Romans to be found in modern-day London.

* * *

The Roman City Wall

One of the largest construction projects carried out by the Romans was the building of a high wall to surround the ancient City of Londinium. It was extended many times during the Roman occupation and was adapted and heightened by others over the years following the Roman departure from Britain. The wall was roughly semi-circular in shape, with the river forming its southern boundary. As well as a means of defence, its purpose would probably have been to control the passage of goods and people.

The Romans built the wall using more than 80,000 tons of ragstone, a type of hard grey limestone found in Kent. It included more than twenty bastions, from which Roman soldiers could defend their positions, mostly on the eastern side, and with a large fort incorporated into the north-west section. Parts of the wall have survived, and today can still be seen around the outskirts of the City of London.

One of the most impressive sections of the wall still remaining is in gardens close to the Tower of London. The lower part was built by the Romans in about AD 200. On the inside, the wall was originally reinforced by an earth rampart. In Roman times it stood about 20 feet high. Today it is more like 30 feet. The original Roman wall having crumbled to about 12 feet from the ground, the rest of the wall above was added in medieval times.

In the Roman era this section would have included several bastions. A deep ditch on the external face would

The remains of the Roman Wall at Tower Hill, close to the Tower of London.

A statue believed to be of the Roman emperor Trajan stands in front of the ancient Roman wall today.

have provided extra defence and made the wall look even higher from the outside. In front of the wall stands a statue believed to be of the Roman Emperor Trajan, who reigned from AD 98–117.

In medieval times this area was also the location for the Tower Hill scaffold, where dangerous criminals and dissidents were beheaded, among them Lord Lovat, a Scottish Jacobite who was convicted of treason and beheaded in 1747, the last man in England to be executed in this way. No remains of this gruesome landmark now remain.

Find your way around the perimeter of what was once the City's boundary and you'll find many other fragments of the Roman wall.

There is a small section in a courtyard in Cooper's Row, where the Roman section is about 12 feet, high with a medieval section added. In this part of the wall, you can still see small openings, called loopholes, where archers once stood to fire their arrows at an approaching enemy.

In Vine Street, the road runs into a small square, where there is a section of the wall, including the base of a bastion tower, which in the fourth century would have held catapults and firing positions for archers.

In Dukes Place, you need to descend a pedestrian subway to see the bottom part of the wall, which in Roman times would have been at ground level.

Not surprisingly perhaps, there is a road in this vicinity actually called London Wall. If you walk along it you will be roughly following the outside edge of the wall at this point, albeit not exactly along the track, since this road was widened in the mid-twentieth century.

Nevertheless, you will come upon All Hallows Church, the oldest church in the City of London. The present building was designed and built in 1767, replacing an older church that dated back to the twelfth century. The peculiarity of

The Guild Church of All Hallows-on-the-Wall, built on the foundations of the Roman Wall.

the newer church is that its vestry was built into the foundations of the old Roman Wall. Its shape echoes the semi-circular design of one of the wall's bastions.

Not far away, the church of St Alphege was built onto the Roman Wall, although what remains today in St Alphege Gardens is largely the medieval remains that were built on top of the now vanished Roman Wall.

Further on, St Giles Cripplegate is one of the few remaining medieval churches remaining in the City of London. Although most of the stonework of the wall that can be seen here is from the medieval period, it does mark the position of the old Roman fort that stood at this location. Nearby is what remains of a large medieval tower, which marks the north-western corner of the old Roman Wall and the fort that was part of it.

Remains of other towers, built on the foundation of the old Roman Wall, are also to be found nearby at Barber-Surgeon's Hall and the Museum of London.

Not far away, in Noble Street, a long stretch of the City Wall can still be seen, incorporating much of the original Roman structure at its base.

Although some of what remains to be seen today is medieval rather than Roman, the original Roman Wall still lies as the heart of most of the later medieval building works.

* * *

What's Left of Bishopsgate

There were originally eight gates in the Roman London Wall, each allowing access to the City. One of the most famous of these was Bishopsgate, which marked the start of a road the Romans called Ermine Street. The road ran from what is now London to Lincoln, and then on to York. The Roman gate on this site was rebuilt in 1471, and again in 1735, before being demolished in 1760. At this time, it was a place where the heads of criminals were displayed on spikes.

Today there is nothing left of what was once an important entrance to the City – but there is a small memorial to it, if you know where to look. At 110 Bishopsgate, there stands a commercial skyscraper called the Heron Tower. Look up at the facia above one of the shops on the ground floor, and you'll discover a bishop's mitre built high up into the stonework.

The mitre indicates that the Heron Tower now stands on the site of the old Bishopsgate.

* * *

The Remains of a Roman Wharf

Walking through the arch in the tower of St Magnus the Martyr church in Lower Thames Street, which once led to the pedestrian footway of Old London Bridge, you'll notice a stump of extremely ancient wood. This is actually part of a Roman wharf that would have stood close to one of the old wooden Roman bridges. The stump has been dated back to AD 75, and was excavated at nearby Fish Street Hill in 1931. The distance between its point of discovery and the banks of the Thames today shows how far the river banks have moved during two millennia.

Remains of an old Roman wharf stand within the arch of St Magnus the Martyr church.

* * *

The Grave in the Gherkin

In the heart of London's financial district, stands a 180-foot high, 40-storey skyscraper. Named for its address, it is officially called 30 St Mary Axe, but its unofficial name that most have known it by since its opening in 2004, is the Gherkin, due to its unique shape. It is one of the City's most widely recognised examples of contemporary architecture. So it might come as a surprise to learn that a building that is so well known for being an icon of the modern age should house a Roman grave at its base.

The grave houses the remains of an unknown teenage Roman girl who was buried at this site sometime from 350 to AD 400, dates that were ascertained from the designs of pottery that was discovered nearby. Her original burial, with her head to the south and her arms

To the spirits of the dead the unknown young girl from Roman London lies buried here

DIS MANIBVS PVELLA INCOGNITA LONDINIENSIS HIC SEPVLTA EST

A Roman grave is marked at the base of the Gherkin.

The building known as the Gherkin, one of modern London's most iconic landmarks.

folded across her body, would have been close to the very edge of the City as it was in Roman times.

Her skeleton was discovered in 1995, during excavation work for the building of the Gherkin, then to be known as the Swiss Re Building. For the next twelve years it was kept in the nearby Museum of London. In 2007, her remains were again laid to rest close to her original grave.

Today an inscription in stone at the burial site states, in Latin: *Dis manibvs pvella incognita Londoninensis hic sepvlta est.* The words translate as: To the spirits of the dead, the unknown girl from Roman London lies buried here.

* * *

Where Gladiators Fought in London

Within about thirty years of the Romans establishing Londinium as a major city of the British Isles, they built an open-air amphitheatre in the City. Here, animal fights, gladiatorial combats and criminal executions took place in front of thousands of spectators, seated on tiered wooden benches. The remains of this mighty edifice can still be seen.

The amphitheatre is situated in the basement of the Guildhall in Gresham Street, and is free to visit. Established in the nineteenth century to display a collection of art treasures deemed worthy of the country's capital city, visitors today can see exhibitions of paintings that cover eras from 1670 to the twenty-first century.

The Guildhall is a Grade I listed building, which was opened in 1411. Walking towards the building across Guildhall Yard, you'll notice a wide curved line of dark stone embedded in the lighter stone that covers the ground. This marks the perimeter of the amphitheatre, which is actually situated about 25 feet below the ground. It is accessible from the art gallery inside the building.

Markings in the stone at Guildhall Yard indicate the outline of the old Roman amphitheatre.

The amphitheatre was built by the Romans in about AD 70 and remained intact until the invaders left Britain in the fifth century, when it fell into ruins. Much of it was used for building materials as

What remains of the Amphitheatre beneath the Guildhall Art Gallery.

smaller settlements grew up around the area until the first Guildhall was built on the site. Archaeologists discovered the amphitheatre in 1988, while working on the new Guildhall Art Gallery.

Descending from the art gallery today, it is possible to see the remains of the amphitheatre's original walls and drainage system. To help you visualise what it must have looked like in Roman times, the modern technology of a digital projection system fills in the gaps in the ancient ruin.

* * *

The London Stone

In Cannon Street, the wall of a building opposite Cannon Street station has a decorative grill made of Portland stone set into it right down at pavement level. From a distance, it looks like nothing more than a piece of decorative ornamentation. But get down to its level and peer through the stone grill and you'll see that it's there to protect what appears to be a small lump of stone. This is the London Stone, often quoted as being of Roman origin.

Much of its history is lost in the mists of time and much of what you hear quoted is either guesswork or little more than myth. What

The London Stone, behind a grill in Cannon Street.

is pretty much certain is that the stone that exists today is only the tip of a monument that was originally much larger. It was made from a carbonate rock called oolitic limestone, which was first brought to Britain by the Romans, who used it for building and sculpturing. Its original location was in front of a building, often identified as the Roman Governor's palace, which was located where Cannon Street station now stands.

The stone was also known to be a significant monument in Saxon times, went on to be damaged by, yet survive, the Great Fire of London, which destroyed most of the surrounding buildings, was moved several times during its lifetime, survived two world wars, and much more besides. Legends have also grown up around the stone proclaiming that London's very existence would be in jeopardy if the stone were ever destroyed. Other legends claim it to be the stone from which King Arthur pulled his sword *Excalibur*.

The truth is that no one really knows the origins or the purpose of the London Stone, but there it remains behind its stone grill in Cannon Street, and there's every chance that it is actually a small piece of Roman London history.

Chapter 14

Egyptian London

The British Museum in Great Russell Street houses one of the world's largest collections of Egyptian artefacts outside of Egypt itself. And it's not alone. The Petrie Museum at University College London in Malet Place has on show a huge collection of Egyptology. But you don't have to visit a museum to see evidence of Egypt in London. If you know where to look, it's all around you.

* * *

Cleopatra's Needle

Cleopatra's Needle stands on its plinth on the north bank of the river Thames between Waterloo and Hungerford bridges. It's actually an obelisk nearly 70 feet high, weighing more than 200 tons, covered in Egyptian hieroglyphics and flanked on each side by an enormous sphinx. But it's not all it seems.

Although the Needle dates back to Ancient Egypt around 3,500 years ago, it actually has very little to do with Queen Cleopatra, who was on the throne about 1,400 years after the monument was created. What's more, the sphinxes are neither ancient nor Egyptian. They are Victorian and English.

Cleopatra's Needle, on the north bank of the river Thames.

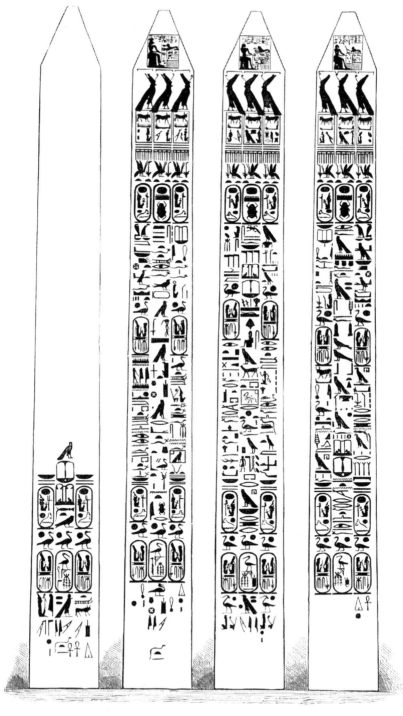

The hieroglyphics on the four faces of the Needle are in honour of Thutmose III and Ramesses II.

Ancient history

The obelisk that has come to be known as Cleopatra's Needle was carved and built for Thutmose III, the sixth pharaoh of the Egyptian eighteenth dynasty. Some of the hieroglyphics praise Thutmose; others were added 200 years later to celebrate the military victories of Ramesses the Great.

It stood in Heliopolis for nearly 1,500 years, until 12 BC, eighteen years after the death of Cleopatra. The Romans, who were by then ruling over Egypt, shifted it to Alexandria, where it was erected in the Caesareum, a temple that had been built by Cleopatra in honour of Julius Caesar and Mark Antony, both of whom had been her lovers. This is the only tangible connection between the monument and the name of the Egyptian Queen.

The events that brought the Needle to London began in 1878, when, during the Battle of the Nile, Napoleon's fleet was ambushed and defeated by English warships led by Lord Nelson. Plans were made to bring the Needle to England to celebrate the victory, but it didn't happen. In 1820, in recognition of not just Nelson, but also the success of British troops under Sir Ralph Abercrombie during the Battle of Alexandria, Egyptian ruler Sudan Muhammad Ali presented the monument to the British nation.

The problem for the British Government was that the country could not afford the resources to pay for its transportation.

The voyage to London

It was English surgeon, dermatologist and philanthropist Sir William James Erasmus Wilson who put up the cash to pay for the Needle to be brought to England. Encased in a wrought iron cylinder that was turned into an ocean-going vessel on the seashore of Alexandria, it was given the name *Cleopatra* and towed behind a ship called the *Olga*.

Tragedy struck in the Bay of Biscay, when the *Cleopatra* had to be cut adrift in a storm. Six men from the *Olga* lost their lives when their boat was swamped during an attempt to rescue their fellow crew members from the *Cleopatra*. Today, their lives are commemorated in a plaque on the side of the monument.

The *Cleopatra* on its way to Britain, towed by the *Olga*.

The Needle, still encased in its cylinder, was later spotted by a Glaswegian steamer and towed to Spain for repairs before a tug boat was sent from England to tow it home. It eventually made land at Gravesend in Kent, four months after leaving Egypt.

Raising the Needle

Erasmus Wilson favoured Parliament Square as a location for the Needle and a wooden model was erected there to give an idea of what it might look like. The final decision, however, was to erect it on the Thames Embankment. As the Needle was towed on its final trip from Gravesend, along the Thames and into the heart of London, a huge wooden structure was erected at the side of the river. It comprised four 50-foot high, diagonally braced posts, at the base of which the obelisk, stripped from its iron cylinder, was inserted.

The machinery for placing the obelisk into position on the Thames Embankment.

Hydraulic jacks were used to raise the horizontal monument to a point where it could be swung through 90 degrees to an upright position and lowered onto its base.

The Victorian Sphinxes

This was at a time when Londoners were showing a great deal of interest in Ancient Egypt. So it's not surprising to find that the Victorians decided to build their own sphinxes to stand each side of Cleopatra's Needle. They were designed by English architect George John Vulliamy, who was also responsible for the bronze pedestal on which the Needle stood, as well as lamp posts along the Embankment, still there today, with dolphins entwined around them. He also designed benches adjacent to the Needle whose armrests resembled winged sphinxes.

The huge sphinxes were cast in bronze with hieroglyphic inscriptions added that translated as 'the good god, Thutmose III given life'. The sphinxes' original purpose was to stand guard over the Needle, in which case, they should be facing outwards and away from

One of the two Victorian sphinxes that flank the Needle.

the monument. In fact, both face the Needle, since Queen Victoria thought that position to be more aesthetically pleasing.

Scars and shrapnel holes on the Needle's pedestal and the bases of the sphinxes are the result of a bomb dropped nearby during the First World War. It was the first London monument to be damaged during this war, giving support to some who believe that Cleopatra's Needle is cursed with bad luck.

The arm rests of seats along the Embankment close to the Needle are made in the form of winged sphinxes.

* * *

The South London Sphinxes

At the Louvre Museum in Paris, close to the entrance to the Egyptian section, there stands a huge sphinx, one of the largest of its type outside of Egypt. It dates back to beyond 2600 BC and was discovered in 1825 among the ruins of the Temple of Amun. Today, it is one of the French museum's top attractions.

One of the sphinxes still standing in South London's Crystal Palace Park.

But you don't have to journey to France to see something similar, because there are life-size copies of that same sphinx in a South London park.

When the Great Exhibition that was staged in Hyde Park ended in October 1851, the Crystal Palace, which housed it, was dismantled and rebuilt at Sydenham in South London, where it dominated an impressive landscape of parkland.

Wide terraces linked the Palace to the park and six huge sphinxes, each one modelled on the Great Sphinx of Tanis, now standing in the Louvre, were arranged in three pairs to stand either side of staircases leading to the terraces. The Crystal Palace burnt down in 1936, but the parkland in which it stood remains. The sphinxes are among the more impressive remnants that have survived from the Victorian era and can today still be seen at one end of Crystal Palace Park.

✳ ✳ ✳

The Carreras Factory Cats

In the 1920s, spurred on greatly by archaeologist Howard Carter's 1922 expedition which uncovered the tomb of Tutankhamen, English architects went through a phase of designing Egyptian style buildings

Replicas of the original black cats standing outside the former Carreras Tobacco Company factory.

and ornamentation. At the same time, the Egyptian cigarette industry began to boom. As a result, many non-Egyptian tobacco companies started to adopt Egyptian-type designs in their advertising.

So when the Carreras Tobacco Company opened for business in 1928 in Mornington Crescent, it did so in a building whose exterior was inspired by the Egyptian temple of the cat god Bubastis. As well as a huge solar disc in tribute to the sun god Ra, the building also featured two enormous Egyptian style cats each side of the main entrance.

Today the building is an office block known as Greater London House, whose builders removed the Egyptian idolatry in 1961. Replicas of the cats, however, were placed back in position in the 1990s, and it is these that adorn the building today.

* * *

Egypt in Islington

From 1801 to 1841, the population of Islington, then a North London parish, grew fivefold, leading to an explosion in house building. The houses, on which building began towards the end of the 1820s, were grand, with Ionic pilasters on walls and Doric columns on doorways.

Miniature sphinxes and Egyptian obelisks stand in front of a row of houses in Islington.

As building continued into the 1830s and then the 1840s, architect William Dennis designed a terrace in the parish's Richmond Avenue, with entrances influenced by the Victorian fondness for all things Egyptian.

That's why most of the houses between 46 and 72 Richmond Avenue, Islington have small sphinxes and obelisks that look like truncated versions of Cleopatra's Needle guarding their front doors.

* * *

The Egyptian Way Of Death

The Egyptians undoubtedly knew how to build memorials to the dead – and so too did the Victorians. Put the two cultures together and the result is a group of London cemeteries where Egyptian influences proliferate.

In Highgate Cemetery, famous for the graves of the famous, who range from philosopher Karl Marx to humorous writer Douglas

The Egyptian Avenue in Highgate Cemetery.

Adams, there's the Egyptian Avenue. It is identified by a huge vine-covered arch that leads to a passage with vaults containing individual shelves on both sides. Each one was originally purchased by a different family for its exclusive use.

In North London, Abney Park Cemetery in Stoke Newington has an entrance designed in the Egyptian Revival style that was popular in Victorian times, consisting of motifs and imagery associated with Ancient Egypt. Hieroglyphics across the entrance spell out 'Abode of the Mortal Part of Man.'

In West London, Kensal Green Cemetery in Harrow Road has a great many Egyptian style mausoleums within its grounds.

* * *

Ancient Egypt Comes to Sotheby's

Sotheby's is one of the world's premier auction houses, whose history in London dates back to 1744. New Bond Street has been its home since 1917, when its premises moved from the Strand. So what is the significance of the bust of Sekhmet, a lion-headed Egyptian warrior goddess, which dates back to about 1320 BC, and which stands above the auctioneer's entrance?

Reckoned to be London's oldest outdoor bust on public display, this ancient Egyptian monument has been at Sotheby's since the late 1800s, when it was consigned to the auction house as part of a collection of ancient Egyptian artefacts.

The lot that included the bust was sold by the auction house for £40. The buyer, however, never collected his winning lot and the bust was subsequently installed above Sotheby's main entrance, where it remains today.

* * *

And There's More

Here are a few more of the many places where you'll find Egyptian influences in London:

- A sculptured panel on the side of Norway House in Cockspur Street near Trafalgar Square shows a woman holding a ball of thread in front of textile factories and sitting on a seat supported by a sphinx.
- A building in Lothbury, behind the Bank of England, has a balcony supported by sphinxes.
- Wyndham's Theatre in Charring Cross Road has a small winged sphinx sitting close to the roof.
- A building in Cornhill, which was the office of the Commercial Union Assurance Company in the 1930s, shows two sphinxes along its façade.

Once you start looking for Egyptian styles in London architecture and landmarks – particularly those of the Victorian age – you'll find them everywhere.

Curiosity Post Codes

The post codes listed below will help the reader in search of the many London curiosities listed in this book to find their locations.

Abbey Mills Pumping Station: E15 2RW
Abney Road Cemetery: N16 0LH
Adelaide Street: WC2N 4HZ
Admiralty Arch: SW1A 2WH
Albert Bridge: SW11 4QG
Albert Hall chimney: SW7 2AP
Albert Memorial: SW7 2AP
All Hallows Church: EC3R 5BJ
Animals in War memorial: SO23 8AL
Arkley windmill: EN5 3LD
Athenaeum Club: SW1Y 5ER
Barbican: EC2Y 8DS
Barking Fire Bell Gate: IG11 7AX
Bazalgette Memorial: WC2N 6PB
Bear Gardens: SE1 9HA
Birdcage Walk: SW1E 6HQ
Bishopsgate: EC2N 4AY
Bishopsgate Turkish Baths: EC2M 3TJ
Blackfriars Road: SE1 8NY
Bracken House: EC4M 9JA
British Museum: WC1B 3DG
Brixton windmill: SW2 5EU
Brookwood Cemetery: GU24 0BL
Brunel Museum: SE16 4LF
Brydges Place: WC2N 4HP
Cabman's shelter: WC2N 6RQ
Cambridge Circus: WC2H 8AA
Camden Market: NW1 8AF

Canonbury Tower: N1 2NQ
Carlton Terrace: SW1Y 5AF
Chenies Street: WC1E 7ET
Chislehurst Caves: BR7 5NL
Cholera Pump: W1F 9QJ
Cleopatra's Needle: WC2N 6DU
Cloth Fair: EC1A 7JQ
Cornhill devils: EC3V 3PD
Courtlands Estate: TW10 5AT
Covent Garden water clock: WC2H 9AS
Crystal Palace Park: SE19 2GA
Devonshire Street: W1G UK
Dr Johnson's cat: EC4A 3DE
Embankment Gardens: WC2N 6DU
Embassy of Texas: E17 7PF
Euston Lodges: NW1 2EF
Fortnum and Masons: W1A 1ER
Gherkin: EC3A 8EP
Giltspur Street: EC1A 9DD
Globe Theatre: SE1 9DT
Golden Boy of Pye Corner: EC1A 9DE
Goldhawk Road: W12 8HD
Greenwich Foot Tunnel: SE10 9HT
Greenwich Observatory: SE10 8XJ
Guildhall: EC2V 7HH
Guy's Hospital: SE1 9RT
Herons Tower: EC2N 4AY
Hitchcock birthplace memorials: E11 3HU
Hitchcock film mosaics: E11 1HE
Hyde Park Corner: SW1X 7LY
Hyde Park Place: W2 2LH
Kensal Green Cemetery: W10 4RA
Kew Gardens: TW9 3AB
King Edward VII Memorial Park: E1W 3EQ
King's Arms, Borough: SE1 1YT
King's Cross lighthouse: N1 9AL
Lambeth Bridge: SE1 7SG
Law Courts: EC4M 7EH
Leicester Square: WC2H 7LQ

Leinster Gardens: W2 6DR
Lighthouse Methodist Church: E17 8BQ
Lincoln's Inn: WC2A 3TL
Lion Brewery lion: SE1 7PB
Little George Street: SW1P 3AD
Lombard Street: EC3V 9AA
London Bridge station: SE1 9SP
London Necropolis Railway station: SE1 7HR
London Stone: E1 2LX
London Zoo: NW1 4RY
Mandela Way: SE1 5SE
Marble Arch: W1C 1LX
Market Road, Holloway: N7 8DJ
Mayflower pub: SE16 4NF
Mount Pleasant Postal Museum: WC1X 0DL
Mouse statue: EC3M 1DE
New Bond Street: W1S 3SN
No. 1 London: W1J 7NT
Old Bond Street: W1S 4PB
Old Curiosity Shop: WC2A 2ES
Oscar Wilde memorial: WC2N 4HZ
Oxford Street Festival sculptures: W1D 2LJ
Oxo Tower: SE1 9PH
Panyer Alley: EC2V 6AA
Paternoster Square: EC4M 7AG
Petrie Museum: WC1E 6BT
Pickering Place: SW1A 1EG
Policeman's coat hook: WC2H 9NY
Postman's Park: EC1A 4AS
Royal Festival Hall: SE1 8XX
Savoy Hotel: WC2R 0EZ
Selfridges: W1A 1AB
Shell-Mex Clock: WC2R 0DT
Sherlock Holmes pub: WC2N 5DB
Shoreditch Park: N1 6TA
Skylon commemorative plaque: SE1 7PB
Soho Square: W1D 3QE
Southwark Needle: SE1 2SX
St Ethelburga-the-Virgin: EC2N 4AG

St Magnus the Martyr: EC3R 6DN
St Pancras Church: NW1 2BA
St Sepulchre-without-Newgate: EC1A 2DQ
St Bride's Church: EC4Y 8AU
St George the Martyr clock: SE1 1JA
St James's Park: SW1A 2BJ
St Mary's Free School: SE16 4NF
St Pancras Old Church: NW1 1UL
St Paul's Cathedral: EC4M 8AD
Temple Church: EC4Y 7BB
The Monument: EC3R 8AH
Thurloe Square: SW7 2TA
Tower Bridge: SE1 2UP
Tower Hill: EC3N 4DJ
Tower subway: EC3N 4AB
Trafalgar Square: WC2N 5DN
Traffic lights plaque: SW1A 0AA
Trinity Buoy Wharf: E14 0JY
Vauxhall Bridge: SW1V 1AA
Vestry House Museum: E17 9NH
Victoria Park: E3 5TB
Walmer Road: W11 4EP
West Smithfield: EC1A 9JQ
Wimbledon windmill: SW19 5NR
Winchester Palace remains: SE1 9DN
Woolwich Foot Tunnel: SE18 6DX

Picture Credits

Page 2 (top): From The Queen's Empire, Volume 3, Cassell & Co., London, public domain, via Wikimedia Commons.

Page 7: © Memoirs of a Metro Girl, http://memoirsofametrogirl.com.

Page 11: © Robert Lordan, www.blackcablondon.net.

Page 14: By Alexander Williams (own work) (http://www.gnu.org/copyleft/fdl.html), via Wikimedia Commons.

Page 16: © Justin Cormack via Wikimedia Commons.

Page 19: © Jane Amelia Parker, www.janeslondon.com.

Page 22: © Viosan, via Wikimedia Commons.

Page 25: © John Godley.

Page 26 (lower): © Memoirs of a Metro Girl, http://memoirsofametrogirl.com.

Page 28: By Robert Bauer (own work, also on www.robert-bauer.eu), via Wikimedia Commons.

Page 34: © Panhard – via Wikimedia Commons.

Page 37: © Valela via Wikimedia Commons.

Page 38: By James Petts from London, England, via Wikimedia Commons.

Page 39: By Fæ (own work), via Wikimedia Commons.

Page 40: By Kjetil Bjørnsrud (own work), via Wikimedia Commons.

Page 42: © Chris Partridge, ornamentalpassions.blogspot.com.

Page 44: By Alan Stanton (CC BY-SA 2.0, http://creativecommons.org/licenses/by-sa/2.0), via Wikimedia Commons.

Page 49: By Nedueb (own work), public domain, via Wikimedia Commons.

Page 53: © David Carritt, https://lookingforghosts.wordpress.com.

Page 55 (top and lower): Courtesy of James Styles.

Page 61 (right): © Chris Partridge, ornamentalpassions.blogspot.com.

Page 64: By Jack1956 (CC0]), via Wikimedia Commons.

Page 68: By Oxyman (own work) (GFDL, http://www.gnu.org/copyleft/fdl.html), CC-BY-SA-3.0 (http://creativecommons.org/licenses/by-sa/3.0/), via Wikimedia Commons.

Page 69 (top): Courtesy of Victor Keegan's LondonMyLondon.co.uk blog.

Page 70: © Ann Lee for Friends of Windmill Gardens.

Page 71: Courtesy of Wimbledon Windmill Museum.

Page 77: By Tony Hisgett, from Birmingham, UK (Fortnum and Mason clock), via Wikimedia Commons.

Page 79: By Love Art Nouveau (CC BY 2.0, http://creativecommons.org/licenses/by/2.0), via Wikimedia Commons.

Page 84: By Ann Biddle, from UK (Tim Hunkin and Andy Plant's Clock, CC BY 2.0 (http://creativecommons.org/licenses/by/2.0), via Wikimedia Commons.

Page 85: By Martin Pettitt (Flickr: London Zoo, Clock by Tim Hunkin, CC BY 2.0 http://creativecommons.org/licenses/by/2.0), via Wikimedia Commons.

Page 87: By Duncan Harris, from Nottingham, UK (Clocks), CC BY 2.0 http://creativecommons.org/licenses/by/2.0), via Wikimedia Commons.

Page 88 (top): Scan from the original work, public domain, via Wikimedia Commons.

Page 95: © Dr Tony Shaw.

Page 103: By Kleon3 (own work), CC BY-SA 4.0 (http://creativecommons.org/licenses/by-sa/4.0)], via Wikimedia Commons.

Page 104: By Kleon3 (own work), CC BY-SA 4.0 (http://creativecommons.org/licenses/by-sa/4.0), via Wikimedia Commons.

Page 105: Noel Jenkins, CC BY-SA 2.0 (http://creativecommons.org/licenses/by-sa/2.0)], via Wikimedia Commons.

Page 108 (top): Courtesy of Friends of Hyde Park & Kensington Gardens.

Page 109: © Peter Watts.

Page 111: By Mark S. Jobling (Mjobling at en.wikipedia), public domain, via Wikimedia Commons.

Page 113: By Matt Brown from London, England (Mail Rail trains), CC BY 2.0 (http://creativecommons.org/licenses/by/2.0), via Wikimedia Commons.

Page 114: Courtesy of Jason Desporte, General Manager, Chislehurst Caves.

Page 116: From a contemporary postcard.

Page 126: By Targeman (own work), public domain, via Wikimedia Commons.

Page 127: © Bob White.

Page 141: By Iridescenti (own work), GFDL (http://www.gnu.org/copyleft/fdl.html), CC-BY-SA-3.0 (http://creativecommons.org/licenses/by-sa/3.0/), via Wikimedia Commons.

Page 143: By Panhard (own work), GFDL (http://www.gnu.org/copyleft/fdl.html), CC-BY-SA-3.0 (http://creativecommons.org/licenses/by-sa/3.0/), via Wikimedia Commons.

Index